CRITICAL RACE THEORY
AND
THE CHURCH

CRITICAL RACE THEORY
AND
THE CHURCH

A Concise Analysis

Larry E. Ball, M.Div., CPA

VICTORIOUS HOPE
PUBLISHING
Chesnee, South Carolina 29323

"Proclaiming the kingdom of God and teaching those things which concern
the Lord Jesus Christ, with all confidence."
(Acts 28:31)

Critical Race Theory and the Church: A Concise Analysis
© Copyright 2022 by Larry E. Ball

Unless otherwise noted, Scripture references are taken from the New American Standard Bible, (c) 1960, 1962, 1963, 1968, 1971, 1972, 1973, 1975, 1977 by The Lockman Foundation. Used by permission.

Published by Victorious Hope Publishing
P.O. Box 285
Chesnee, SC 29323

Website: www.VictoriousHope.com

Printed in the United States of America

ISBN: 978-1-7343620-7-7

Cover design by Bryan Shackelford

Proofing and editing by Jonathan Williams, Diana Armstrong, and Claire Shackelford

Victorious Hope Publishing is committed to producing Christian educational materials for promoting the whole Bible for the whole of life. We are conservative, evangelical, and Reformed and are committed to the doctrinal formulation found in the Westminster Standards.

Dedication

This book is dedicated to the memory of
two of the greatest theologians of the 20th century:

Dr. Cornelius Van Til (1895–1987)
and
Rev. R. J. Rushdoony (1916–2001)

TABLE OF CONTENTS

INTRODUCTION

This Book is intentionally short. I am able to write long books, but there is no need for that. The time is urgent! Besides, most people don't read books anymore, especially long ones. Most reading today is done on Facebook and Twitter. There are several excellent books on Critical Race Theory (CRT) from a Christian perspective, but I fear they will remain mostly unread. If you are up to it, I do recommend one particular book, *Christianity and Social Justice, Religions in Conflict*, by Jon Harris.[1]

My book is written for three reasons: First, it is short and thus people may be more likely to read it. Secondly, I come from a different cultural and theological perspective than most other Christians as you will see as you read the book (that alone makes this book different). Thirdly, as God gives gifts to men, He seems to have made me a middleman. By this, I mean that I can sit under great scholars and understand what they are saying, and then I can put their ideas into the language of the average guy in the pew. I believe my background prepared me for this.

I have 40 years of experience in the pastorate, a Master's Degree from Westminster Theological Seminary in Philadelphia, and a Bachelor's Degree in mathematics. I am a Certified Public Accountant (CPA) and also an Enrolled Agent with the Internal Revenue Service. I have some educational credentials. I have taught accounting courses on the college level. I have run my own tax business for over 25 years.

On the other hand, I was raised in the coalfields of Appalachia where white people were considered mostly poor, ignorant, and backward. I was raised as a white minority. Some people called us white trash.

---

[1] Jon Harris, *Christianity and Social Justice: Religions in Conflict* (Ann Arbor, Mich: Reformation Zion, 2021). www.reformationzion.com.

I can attest that there was grave poverty among both whites and blacks in the mountains, especially in the coalfields. I witnessed both black and white men walking the railroad tracks looking for lumps of coal that may have fallen off the coal trains. Coal provided heat for the family in the wintertime. This was before the welfare system and EBT food stamps. There were no free-loaders, only survivors. In the early 20th century, miners were often treated like slaves by the mine-owners. My father told me once that miners like him were treated worse than the mules that pulled the coal out of the mines. On occasion, families living in houses owned by the mine-owners were ejected from their homes without anywhere to go. Most of them lived in tents.

When I was a young child, with eight people living in our small home with one bathroom about the size of a closet, there was not much room. I slept with my sister, me at the head of the bed and her at the foot of the bed. The bed was one that my mother retrieved from a trash dump. I remember vividly a rat crawling on our bed during the night.

Thus, I have lived in the world of the underprivileged, and I have lived in the world of the academic elite. Maybe this is one reason I consider myself a middleman.

A summary of the premise of this book is as follows: Neo-Marxism controls the federal government in the United States and the leadership of most of our large cities. It dominates nearly all of the universities and corporate boardrooms in America. It has also infiltrated the church. Critical Race Theory is a child of Neo-Marxism. We are not simply in the middle of a political war, but more importantly a religious war for the soul of our nation. Unless the church awakens from her stupor, our children and our children's children will suffer greatly. However, in the long term there is hope. The Kingdom of God has defeated worse. Christ always wins in the end.

As I proceed through this book, I will first define Critical Race Theory (ch. 1), then look at the biblical origins of terms like equality and equity (ch. 2). I will deal with the myth that races do not exist, and look at why there are differences among the races (ch. 3). This will be followed by a description of the character of Neo-Marxism, as the root of CRT (ch. 4). I will analyze the dangers inherent in the modern evangelical church which in my opinion is unable to deal with CRT (ch. 5). Finally, I will propose a return to an older view of the relationship between the church and civil government which I believe is the only biblical option (ch. 6). I shall wrap up the whole matter with some remarks in the Conclusion. So, let's get started.

Chapter 1
CRITICAL RACE THEORY – WHAT IS IT?

A New Religion

All of life is religious. That is the assumption of this book. Man is created in the image of God, and all that he does reflects this fact. If you drive a truck, you are performing a religious act. If you teach in a school (even a public school), you are performing a religious act. We tend to think of religion as restricted to worship in a church on Sunday morning. Although worship is an important part, religion is much more than that. Therefore, since all of life is religious, all men are religious. This is an operating definition for me. It's what I call a theological presupposition.

The type of religion any man has and which governs all his actions is defined by the god that he trusts. For example, if you believe that there is no god, and man by his own reason can define and solve the problems of life, then you are religious. Reason is your god. Your religion is called Humanism.

If you believe that Democracy adopted in any nation can bring happiness and joy to that society, then democracy is your religion. Your god is "We the People." If 51% of the people's vote determines what is right in any society, the majority vote is your ultimate source of truth. The majority vote is your god. Democracy is your religion. Democracy (actually the concept of a Republic) used to be considered an application of the Christians Faith, but since Christianity is dying in America, a better term now might be Secular Democracy.

Another subtle religion that has been prominent in history is Marxism. The ultimate reference point (or god) in Marxism is equality. It promotes the idea that everyone must be made equal in all facets of life. For example, everyone must wear the same style of clothing (usually drab) to reduce the differences that result from some people looking better dressed than others. Or everyone should share equally in the financial income of their employer. All employees should take home the same amount of money on pay-day, regardless of talent or the amount of production on the job. Income inequality must be ended.

Critical Race Theory (CRT) is a new religion, and yet at the same time, it is an old religion, as are all new religions. It is new in the sense that it uses new words and language that have not been used before. It is old in the sense that it is nothing more than a continuation of the work of Satan in the Garden of Eden to dethrone the authority of God. There are only two religions in this world — Christianity and then everything else. Christ said "he who is not for me is against me." So, either we are followers of Christ or we are against Christ. "Everything else" is a description of those against Christ. Everything else comes in many forms such as Humanism and Secular Democracy. Christ is the way, the truth, and the life, and everything opposed to His Kingship over all things is just Satan tempting us to rebel against God, just as he led Adam and Eve into the sin of defying God.

When we think of religions opposed to Christianity, we tend to think in terms of the big ones like Islam, Judaism, Buddhism, and Hinduism. The Evangelical Church in general is very naive and does not understand the dangers of more subtle religions like Humanism, Secular Democracy, and Marxism. CRT is a new form of Marxism which I call Neo-Marxism. I'll trace this connection in a later chapter.

A Definition of Critical Race Theory
In essence CRT declares the following:
1. All white people (especially old white males) are guilty of the sin of oppression of all races (including all minorities and genders), especially the black race.
2. As guilty sinners, white people need to recognize their guilt, repent, lament, weep, and pay for their sins of the past.

3. Slavery in the 18th and 19th centuries and the Jim Crow laws in both the 19th and 20th centuries are the fault of all white men living today in the 21st century.

4. If you are white, you are guilty. Even if you have never mistreated a black person, or belittled them in any way, you still are guilty.

We are told that this new religion demands equality. However, do not be deceived. The ultimate goal of this new religion is equity. Equity is not the same thing as equality. Equality is the principle that we are all equal (I'll expound on this later). Equity is the pursuit of equality by enacting the transfer of wealth, position, and power from the white man to the black man (or non-whites). It is the process or the end result of reshuffling the ownership of assets. Once the CRT religion is in power, it will redistribute the wealth of the white race through the power of the civil government. Also, as it captures American universities and major corporations, it will enforce equity on all of their employees. This process is happening now as you read this book.

This re-distribution of wealth is called reparations or reallocation. Reparations is paying back victims because they have been oppressed by others. By white men paying reparations to the black man, CRT believes the white man will be making some atonement for his sins of the past. Assets, money, power, and position will move from the white man to the black man — and to women, homosexuals, lesbians, transgenders, and others not defined as a white man. The result of this exchange, they believe, will be a new utopia on earth.

If, as a white person, you deny that you are a racist, then you are a liar. If this upsets you then you are fragile. Your fragility[2] is only proof that you are a liar and a racist. Your unwillingness to admit your guilt shows that you are weak. If you want to debate the issue, you are not allowed to do so because you are white, and you have not experienced the life of a black man. You can't understand

---

[2] Robin Diangelo, *White Fragility* (Boston: Boston Press, 2018).

what it means to live on the other side of the tracks. Experience is the supreme interpreter of truth. There is no room for discussion on the matter. If you try to communicate with followers of the CRT religion, the common response is screaming or striking back at you in some form! This is the end result of any attempt to have a dialogue. You are a racist and that is the end of discussion.

What Is Racism?

Racism is despising another race based solely on their skin color or some other physical feature unique to various races. CRT believes that all whites are guilty of racism against blacks and non-whites. They believe that racism is something only white people can commit. Yet, on the contrary, I would argue that the same logic can be used to conclude that CRT proponents are guilty of racism. Since CRT believes that all white people are inherently evil based on the color of their skin, then by definition, they are racist. This used to be called reverse discrimination. Accusations cut both ways. What an irony!

Racism is Systemic

CRT also asserts that racism is a systemic sin because it exists in the institutions and structures of society. Even if you do not harbor racism personally, you would still be guilty because you are white and you participate in the institutions that exist in society. Not only are you an individual person, but you are also part of groups and institutions in our culture.

Racism is systemic in that it pervades all the institutions of society like the public schools, the university, the company you work for, sports, and the white church. It's in everything. It is latent in the system, and if you are white and participate in any of these systems, then you are a racist.

Other Words Used by CRT

Other terms used in the CRT religion are terms like critical theory, social justice, identity politics, and intersectionality.

Critical Theory is a broader term that simply means that it's time to criticize the past. It's time to rewrite history. It's time to refute all that you were taught in school about history. It's time to dismantle the local monuments of some historical figures like Thomas Jefferson and Teddy Roosevelt. Men like these cannot be honored and respected any longer.

History was constructed by white men to further their oppression of minorities; thus, it is corrupt. The most important date in American history is now 1619 because that was supposedly the year that the first blacks were brought to America. This date replaces other important dates like 1607 when the English landed in Jamestown, or 1776 when the Declaration of Independence was written. These dates were chosen by white people to oppress the black man. They marginalize the importance of blacks.

Social Justice Warriors (SJW) tell us that the labor of black slaves is more important than the work of our forefathers who wrote the United States Constitution (even though blacks could neither read nor write at that time). CRT is pursuing one of the goals of Neo-Marxism which is to deconstruct (rewrite) history to create animosity between the races. CRT proponents teach our youth to hate America because these Neo-Marxists believe that the United States historically has been an evil empire.

Social Justice is also a broader term that includes not only the reparations for the suppression of races, but reparations for all minorities including women, homosexuals, and transgenders. The latest acronym that covers most of these oppressed people is LGBTQA+ which stands for lesbians, gay, bisexual, transgender, queer/questioning, and asexual/ally. The last word "ally" means you support the rights of all the others listed. The "+" sign includes any others that may have been overlooked.

Identity politics is the right for everyone to identify himself as he wishes. If you were born as a girl and want to identify as a boy, then that is your prerogative. It is the right in a political world to choose who you want to be. Gender-reassignment surgery should be the choice of every person. Children should be able to obtain this surgery without permission from their parents.

If you are a man and want to marry another man, then that would be your right. The principles set down in the word of God are now irrelevant. We have a new religion dominating our nation. The use of the word "rights" is used in this world to gain power and influence. That's what politics is — the pursuit of power and influence so you can make the rules for society. If you have the power to identify who you want to be, then you are practicing identity politics.

Intersectionality is a term used to describe a person whose life consists of various categories of minority status, all in one person. For example, if you are black, then you are part of a minority group. If you are black and a female, then you are part of two minority groups, black and female. Blackness and the female gender intersect in you as a person. You then are doubly oppressed. If you are black, female, and a lesbian, then you are in a three-fold minority category; and therefore, you are three-fold oppressed. This is what is meant by CRT when it uses the word intersectionality. Intersectionality is an expansion of CRT which includes homosexuals, lesbians, transgenders, and whatever else you might think of. The more minority qualities you have the more oppressed you are.

CRT and Christianity

Critical Race Theory is a religion that has all the components that you find in the Christian Faith. It uses different terminology but it has its own doctrines similar to orthodox Christian tenets like, for example, original sin, guilt, atonement, savior, sanctification, and heaven.

CRT mimics Christianity in many ways. First of all, CRT projects a doctrine of original sin similar to the Christian doctrine of original sin. Original sin in the Christian Faith is the belief that we are all born guilty before God because we derive our existence from Adam. As the old McGuffey's Reader says, "In Adam's fall, we sinned all." This includes the entirety of all mankind. On the contrary, CRT posits original sin in whiteness. Men (and females too) are sinners because they are born white. White babies are racist, even from the womb. They cannot help it. They cannot change it. It is the original sin in CRT.

Since white people in this country owned slaves and some of them made life very difficult for their slaves, then all whites are guilty of that mistreatment. Too, since many white people treated black people unfairly during the Jim Crow era, you are guilty of that sin. Even though most white people living today were not even alive during these eras, and even if your family immigrated to America after all of this, non-blacks are still guilty. If you deny that you are guilty of this original sin, then this only proves that you are a guilty white person.

Another crucial orthodox Christian doctrine is the Atonement. In the Christian Faith the death of Christ on the cross is the only way we can receive the forgiveness of our sins, once and for all. We put our faith in his work, trusting in the sufficiency of his work so that we are forgiven of all of our sins. This is one area where CRT does not mimic the Christian Faith. In CRT there is no way for the white man to completely atone for his sins of oppression. He may start the process of atonement, but he will never finish. He will remain forever guilty. Ultimately, his wealth, power, and position must be redistributed to all minority groups, but even this will not atone for his sins. There must be continual punishment. There is no forgiveness.

CRT has a savior. In orthodox Christianity Jesus Christ is our Savior. He is the one who delivers us from the guilt and power of sin through his own life and death on the cross. In the CRT religion the State is the Savior. Ultimately, the State must oversee the restitution for any damage done. Those who embody the State must use all their power and force to mandate the redistribution of wealth from the white race to minorities. The most powerful tool in their arsenal is the power to tax. A second tool at their disposal is the power of bureaucratic decrees. In the case of large corporations, the most powerful tool to advance CRT is the power to hire, fire, or promote employees to higher positions in the company (or pass over other qualified employees). A black woman who is a lesbian has a ticket to the top.

In the Christian Faith, sanctification is the battle against sin. Christians fight to eliminate sin from their lives (although never successfully in this life). CRT fights to eliminate the power and the influence of the white male. CRT sanctification is the removal of sin from other people, not from the adherents of CRT itself. They have no sin. The white man must become a minority in this country, and he must be marginalized. One way this is done is through illegal immigration. As people from other nations and races cross our southern border without any restraint, then the white Caucasian race will become a minority group. This will be divine justice for the white man because he oppressed others for so long.

Another key doctrine of the Christian Faith is the doctrine of heaven. Heaven is the place where Christians go when they die, awaiting the resurrection of the body and a new heavens and a new earth where righteousness dwells. CRT has its own heaven also, but it has nothing to do with life after death. They don't believe in life after death. Like Marxism (which I shall deal with later), it pursues a heaven on earth. All religions have some type of utopia which they are seeking. For the CRT religion, utopia is the future on this earth when all minority groups share equally the wealth and power of this nation. They teach the religion of Marxism which believes that a day will come when no one will have any more wealth than his neighbor. This is their heaven.

The New Puritanism

Puritanism in modern American history has been identified with intolerant, miserable people. They have been portrayed as very strict moralists who would punish, banish, or even put to death those who disagreed with them. If I were to use the modern view of the Puritans popular in history books, then I would say that the people of the new woke movement (of which CRT is a part) have become exactly what they have projected onto the Puritans. They are basically miserable and discontented people. Proponents of CRT have created what is known as the "Cancel Culture" where the words and actions of everyone different from them are policed. If you call a man who dresses like a woman by the pronoun him, then you are misgendering that person. You may be banned from Twitter and Facebook. You may lose your job. In other words, you may be canceled.

The Cleveland Indians baseball team had to change the use of their mascot name. They are now called the Cleveland Guardians. In the religion of CRT, the name Indians used as a mascot name for a sports team is racism. It is an example of white men belittling or oppressing Indians (red men). The Atlanta Braves are under attack for the use of the name Braves.

Thus, if you speak using terms they do not approve, they will cancel you. They will censor you. They may terminate your employment. They will hurt you economically and financially. They will destroy you. Even the modern portrayal of the Old Puritans does not compare with what I call the intolerant views of these modern New Puritans. The First Amendment to the United States Constitution guaranteeing the right of free speech has essentially been canceled. Sadly, the church has either adopted this new religion, or she remains silent.

Sometimes, the word "Wokeism" is used to describe the movement of CRT. This term implies that you need to be awakened from your ignorance about the racial oppression that exists in your world. You have been asleep.

Another phrase that is often used to describe the cancel culture is *virtue-signaling*. Wokeism defines morality, and if you say anything contrary to their beliefs then they will tell you that you are wrong. In so doing they are telling you that they have a corner on morality. They are virtuous and you are not. They will signal you — or let you know. This is virtue-signaling.

Courageous Blacks

Before I close this chapter, I need to make one more point. It seems that the major propagators of CRT are white people. Most of them are professors on the university level. Their most common converts are students from upper middle-class white families. I believe the reason they are so vulnerable is because they have lost the Christian faith, and are therefore so easily manipulated by guilt. Where there is no law of God or cross of Christ, man becomes a boatload of guilty feelings without a rudder. When other religions offer a way to deal with this guilt, these people will quickly jump on board. CRT is one of those religions ready to provide a healing ointment for the guilt-ridden conscience.

Actually, some of the best critics of CRT are black people. For example, Dr. Voddie Bachman has written an excellent book on the topic.[3] Candace Owens is a black American woman who is a talk-show host, a political commentator, and an activist. She is very articulate. Dr. Carol Swain, a former law professor at Vanderbilt University, is another black woman who is an outspoken critic of CRT. Essentially, when you begin to look for blacks opposed to CRT there are multitudes of black leaders who understand the issues and who speak about its dangers. Sadly, these black leaders are often called "white supremacists" with black faces and with white-racists words coming out of their mouths.

Conclusion

CRT has only become a public issue in recent years, although it has been brewing in major universities for decades. The white-black relationship in America in my lifetime and in my circles has in general been very good. I think most people from both races believe in dealing with each other in a very kind and respectful way. CRT is creating a race war in the United States.

It is fair to say that most blacks in America are opposed to CRT. Only among the elite in the universities, and now in corporate America (whose board members mostly graduated from those elite universities), has CRT been popular. The problem is what starts at the top will eventually drain to the bottom. What begins in the universities gradually will become ingrained in the people as a whole if there is no pushback. Pushback is no longer allowed on the

---

[3] Voddie T. Baucham, Jr., *Fault Lines: The Social Justice Movement and Evangelicalism's Looming Catastrophe* (Washington, D.C.: Salem, 2021).

campuses of American universities. Any opposition has been canceled.

The root belief of CRT is that all distinctions must be done away with including race, gender, and economic status. We must all be equal in every way. It will be their heaven, but if you are a white man, then it may very well become your hell. Equality and equity are their new gods. We shall examine these terms in the next chapter.

Chapter 2
EQUALITY AND EQUITY

Getting to the Roots of CRT

I had the privilege of going to college. Not everyone has enjoyed this blessing. I majored in mathematics, and I am deeply thankful for being able to study this particular discipline (it's called a discipline because it takes a huge amount of hard work and self-discipline to conquer it — and no one ever really conquers it). I found the study of mathematics to be fascinating. There is much mystery in mathematics, and there are intriguing maneuvers in "doing mathematics." However, I believe what I learned most from my study of mathematics was how to think.

I learned the importance of exact definitions. I learned how to trace ideas back to their origins. I learned how to prove certain theories by tracing a mathematical equation back to fundamental assumptions (axioms) that we all accept. I learned how to start with a simple idea and build it into a complex system, and then reverse direction and go back to the simple idea.

I'm a little like the child who is always asking why. I want to see how and why things work. I never just accepted a mathematical equation at face value. I always wanted to know why it was true. What's behind what we see? Upon what fundamental axioms was it built? Prove it!

I carried this process of thought over into my life in general (also into my theological studies). I always want to know why something is true and how can it be proven. Where did this come from? Why do people believe this? For example, if someone tells me that democracy is the best form of civil government that has ever existed on earth, then my first request will be to ask him to define what he means by the term democracy. Secondly, tell me where the idea originated, and thirdly prove that it is the best form of government. Oh my! I always have a multitude of fundamental questions before I can rest and accept statements that other people make. In any conversation with others, my mind is constantly gyrating, almost out of control as I think about these things.

Back Before Time

To understand our topic, we need to go back in time and try to understand where it came from. What are its origins? Even as important (as understanding the origins are) we need to comprehend the terms that are used to define it. You see, I have to go back to axioms (origins) to try to make sense of this whole religion. Again, that's because of my mathematics training. Two of the most important terms in the definition of CRT are the words *equality* and *equity*.

Actually, the term equality is being replaced by the term equity as the mantra in the CRT religion. The word equity is important to them because the movement is trying to remove inequity from this earth. My goal in this chapter is to demonstrate that both equality and inequity exist in the very nature of God. Inequity is the problem they are trying to cure. We need to understand the origin and definition of these words since they are basic to the definition of CRT. Then we can move on to the movement of CRT itself. Do you follow me? This is the way I think.

So, let's go way back. I mean way back. Not just to the Fall of Adam and Eve in the Garden of Eden, or even to the beginning of the world at creation, but let's go back before the world was made and see what we can learn first about God himself. Let's go back before time, when only God Himself existed. CRT is built upon a fundamental concept of equality and equity, and to understand CRT, we (or at least I do) need to go back to the very beginning to see what equality and equity (and inequity) looked like in the personhood of God himself.

Defining Words

Before we go back before time was created by God, I need to say something about language and words. In order to understand

CRT, we also need to understand something about how we perceive the meaning of words. Oh my, here I am going back to definitions!

My point is that words in themselves mean very little, if anything. For words to be meaningful, there must be a context. Some of the words I shall be examining in this book are words like equality, equity, and race. What do those words mean? Well, without context, they don't mean much at all.

For example, the word *fire* is a word that we all understand to some degree, but by itself, it does not convey the concept of either good or bad (the words *good* and *bad* need to be defined too, but I don't have time in this book). A fire that is used on the kitchen stove to prepare eggs is a good thing (if you like eggs). It's the context that gives it meaning. A fire that is destroying a forest conveys a negative concept. Thousands of acres of trees, houses, and animals being destroyed is not a good thing. It's tragic. My point is that a word without a context is mostly useless to convey meaning. Give it context and we have a debate.

Likewise, words like equality, equity, and race are in themselves harmless. Give them a context and in our day, look for a fight. For example, if I say equality of income should be mandated by the United States government, someone will be adamantly opposed. If I say that all men should receive equal treatment before the law of God, then there will not be much disagreement (however things are changing fast). Don't be misled by words without context. As I explore the origins of the debate surrounding CRT, I will be giving contexts to words that are crucial as we examine the movement itself.

Back to the Beginnings

Now, back to the beginning, or rather back to *before* the beginning. In the beginning God created the heavens and the earth (Gen 1:1). However, the Bible tells us a number of things about God before He created the world in which we live. God was there before the world was made. God is eternal.

Now, what does this have to do with CRT? My first point is before time the word *equality* and the word *inequity* are useful to reveal the nature and character of God. These are concepts that existed before the world was made. The words equality and inequity are comparison words and must have at least two participants in order to have meaning. In the Trinity we have three persons, so therefore we can discuss the meaning of both equality and inequity in the Godhead. If God's nature consists of equality and inequity, then that gives those two words both meaning and value for our day.

Equality in the Trinity

Hang on! The Trinity is as follows. There is only one God, but He exists in three persons, each person is separate from the other, and yet each is equally God.[4] God the Father is not the Son nor the Holy Spirit. God the Son is not the Father nor the Holy Spirit. God the Holy Spirit is not the Father nor the Son. They are three distinct persons. Yet, there is only one God. This is called the doctrine of the Trinity which has been a hallmark belief of the church down through the ages. It's something we cannot understand fully, but yet the church believes that it is clearly taught in the Bible. For my purposes in this book, the main point here is that all three persons of the Trinity are equal in power, holiness, truth, and all are equally eternal. There is equality in the very nature of God himself. That is the origin of the word equality.

This is the first concept of the term *equality* that we find not just in history, but before history began. In its context we know this to be a good thing because God is good. This also tells us of the nature of God and the relationship between the three persons of the Trinity. There is equality between the three persons. There is diversity in their names and what they do, yet there is perfect love and contentment in the personhood of God. My point here is that equality is, and can be, a good thing in the right context. It existed in the very nature of God before the world began.

---

[4] See *The Athanasian Creed*.

Equality Turned Bad

Now, for a moment, let's move on beyond creation to the Fall in the Garden of Eden. God told Adam not to eat of the tree "in the middle of the Garden" (Gen. 3:3). Satan convinced Eve to eat of the tree with the temptation that "you will be like God" (Gen 3:5). In other words, you shall be equal with God. In this context the word equal is used for evil. Equality here is a bad thing. Equality in this context implies moving out of your appointed position and claiming something that does not belong to you. Equality here is rooted in the sin of jealousy. Adam and Eve both ate of the fruit seeking equality with God, and sin and death entered the world, and so death spread to all men. In this context jealousy created dissatisfaction which resulted in Adam and Eve seeking equality with God. The Fall teaches us that Adam and Eve believed that God must share his knowledge, power, and truth with man in order for there to be equality. Again, equality in this context is evil. Remember, the definition of a word depends on its context.

Thus, in the context of the very nature of God as He existed before the foundation of the world, equality is a good word. However, in the context of the Fall where Adam and Eve sought equality with God, it is a bad word. Adam and Eve were not the fourth and fifth persons in the Trinity. They were creatures under the authority of God Himself. They were attempting to move up the ladder (so-to-speak) which was impossible. This attempt at equality brought destruction and death on all mankind, and made the coming of Christ necessary to deliver us from the curse of sin.

Equality Among All

Before I conclude this discussion on Equality, I should mention that there are at least three ways in which all men, all races, and all nations are equal. First, we all descend from Adam and thus we all inherit sinfulness. "Therefore, just as through one man sin entered into the world, and death through sin, and so death spread to all men, because all sinned..." (Rom. 5:12). Secondly, as sinners in need of salvation, the gospel offer is equally available for all men. We find this clearly taught in Galatians, "There is neither Jew nor

Greek, there is neither slave nor free man, there is neither male nor female: for you are all one in Christ Jesus" (Gal. 3:28). Thirdly, the Bible gives a very clear message to those who administer the law of God in Deuteronomy 1:17, "Show no partiality in judging; hear both small and great alike. Do not be intimidated by anyone, for judgment belongs to God." God is not a respecter of persons (Acts 3:28). Regardless of race, nationality, or sex, all people are to be judged equally by the law.

Inequity in the Trinity

Now, back before the beginning of time. Whereas we find equality in the Trinity, we also find inequity in the Trinity. The word *equality* refers to the status of the three persons of the Trinity who are equals in their being (sometimes this is called the ontological relationship), but the word *inequity* refers to the three persons of the Trinity who are *unequal* in their responsibilities (sometimes this is called the economic relationship). By unequal, I don't mean that one is more valuable than the other. Rather, I mean that the tasks assumed by each one are different. Each person of the Trinity has his own particular function in the work of salvation. The Father sends the Son to die on the cross for his people. The Son gladly takes upon himself the existence of a man and is crucified for the forgiveness of their sins. The Holy Spirit completes the work of the Father and the Son by acting in the life of believers. The Holy Spirit creates faith in them and enables them to persevere until they reach heaven's glory. Since the word inequity can be used to describe the economic relationship of the Trinity, it is a perfectly legitimate concept for us as well.

It's a little like what economists call the division of labor. Although each person is equal in being, yet each person in the Trinity has a separate and specific function in the accomplishment of salvation. Each one, carrying out his responsibility, enables the one goal to be completed.

Inequity Among Men

As there are differences in the three persons of the Godhead, there are also differences in each of his creatures. We are not all the same, no more than the three persons of the Trinity are the same. As we shall see, even though there is equality in all of us as image-bearers of God, there are also differences in us as individuals, as well as differences in us as races and nations.

Since equity can also refer to wealth, the word inequity can refer to the differences among us regarding the wealth we own, just as each of the three persons of the Trinity had a particular and separate wealth that was used in the salvation of men. The reward of our tasks completed here on earth is usually defined by words like *assets* or *property* which is in many ways equivalent to the word equity. Equity is another name for the assets or the property we own. Inequity, therefore, refers to the amount of separate and different wealth we each own that mostly results from our labors here on earth. Wealth differs among men. *There is inequity in the Trinity and there is also inequity here on earth.*

The definition of wealth usually refers to property or money, but it can also refer to other entities such as power and position. If you have been productive over the years, you should have built up some equity in your life. It may take the form of the house that you own (or partially own), or the money you have in the bank. It may also take the form of the position you hold at your job, or the power you have over other people. The knowledge you have that enables you to do your job well is a type of equity. Respect for you as a person is a form of equity. A good reputation is equity. Children as a blessing can be viewed as a form of equity. Good health is wealth and therefore it is a form of equity. Forgiveness in Christ can be viewed as a form of wealth or equity.

Although the Bible teaches us to be content with the necessities of life, most people in this world strive to build as much equity as they can. We enjoy having things like nice homes, vacations, money in the bank, and many other assets. We enjoy a promotion at our job. We enjoy praise from others for a job well-done. We enjoy our children and grandchildren. We enjoy our spouses. We enjoy the fellowship of the saints at church. These are all forms of wealth. Or, in other words, these are all forms of equity. Looking at it from another angle, they also demonstrate inequity. Again, we do not all have the same amount of equity.

The Origins of Inequity

Different individuals, families, races, and nations have different amounts of equity for a number of various reasons. It's a complex world. I shall list a few reasons why equity varies among us, but I'm sure there are many more. Why is there inequity in life?

1. *The most common source of inequity is hard work.* Sometimes, the result of diligence is called sweat equity. Generally, working hard and doing a good job pays dividends. Some people work two or three jobs at a time. They give all their attention to their work, try to remain focused, and do not waste any time. They are dependable to do the job well and finish on time. Often, they will go beyond the demands of their employer. They normally are rewarded with a larger paycheck or a promotion to a higher position. They add equity not only to the company but to their own wealth. However, laziness can make a man poor and will generally produce major inequities in life.

2. *Inequity can result from being raised in a good home.* By a "good home," I mean a traditional Christian home where a mother and father are present and the family goes to church. This often gives security to children, teaches them that there is a God who is watching them, and that there is a right and a wrong. Such children are then in a better position to pursue high-paying careers without all the dysfunction that comes from the absence of a good home. With the decrease in traditional nuclear homes, we will continue to see more inequity in this world.

3. *Inequity can come from God-given abilities.* Some people can write wonderful novels, and others can hardly write. Some people have great memories and others don't. Some people can run fast and others can hardly walk. As God gives gifts to some and not to others, this creates a difference in equity. With differences in abilities come differences in rewards.

4. *Inequity can come from inheritance.* If your parents leave you a large sum of money or even a farm, then you have increased your equity. However, remember that your parents probably scraped and saved all their lives to build this equity. It was passed to you upon their death, and you are now a man with a great amount of equity. For those who inherit little to nothing, this also creates inequity in this world.

5. *Inequity can even be expanded to include physical characteristics.* By this I mean concepts like beauty in females and strength and height in men. Have you ever noticed the reaction when a beautiful young girl or a tall handsome young man walks into the office? Physical appearance, even though we might not like to admit it, is a part of the equity that people are born with.

6. *Opportunity can be wealth or a type of equity.* A young white boy with a high SAT score from a traditional nuclear family who has been taught to work hard while going to school has an advantage in accumulating equity. A black teenager raised in urban Chicago probably will not have the same opportunity as a white boy.

7. *The same is true not only of races, but also within the same race.* A white teenager raised in drug-infested Appalachia will not have the same opportunity as a white teenager raised in an upscale neighborhood in a large suburban city, where the family drives a nice car and attends church. I'm not trying to throw any guilt trips here on anyone. I'm only trying to demonstrate the origins of inequity.

8. *Sometimes mere providence results in inequity.* For example, purchasing the right stock at the right time. Or, having a cousin as the head of the department at the local industry who will hire you because you are related.

9. *Inequity may be the result of theft.* Let's be honest and not sugar-coat everything. Sometimes, people steal what belongs to others. This creates inequity. The reader surely knows exactly what I mean here.

As I said, there is a multitude of reasons why we all have different amounts of equity in this life — why there is inequity. I can't list them all here, but the main point is to define what equity

and inequity are and to show why the amount of equity varies
among people.

Inequity and Covetousness

The problem in a sinful world is that men tend to be jealous of
others who have more equity than they have. This is why God gave
us one of the Ten Commandments which says "Thou shalt not
covet." It is a commandment because we tend to compare ourselves
with other people who have more equity than we have. We tend to
become discontented and depressed. Or we may compare ourselves
with those who have less equity than we have and become proud.

Most people admire others who work hard and gain equity,
even if the other person's success in life exceeds their own, and
regardless of their race or color. We especially admire hard work.
If a man works very hard and is richly rewarded for his labor, then
we should not have a problem with that. Even if God decides to give
others talents that we don't have, we should not have a problem
with that.

God does give people different talents and gifts. I'm glad that
when I have a toothache that God gives certain unique gifts and
opportunities to my dentist. He makes my pain go away. The world
is very efficient because God gave different gifts to different people.
When I have a bad water leak in my kitchen, I am just as thrilled
with my plumber. He too makes my pain go away.

Inequity and the Church

It's the same way in the Church. There are a variety of gifts, but
one God. Paul describes the variety of gifts in 1 Corinthians 12 when
he compares it to the body. The body has many parts: eyes, ears,
nose, feet, and hands. All differ in function and all are equally
important. No one member should consider himself above the
others.

Paul goes on to say that when one member thinks too highly of
himself, he needs to learn a lesson, "On the contrary, it is much
truer that the members of the body which seem to be weaker are
necessary; and those members of the body which we deem less

honorable, on these we bestow more abundant honor, and our less presentable members become much more presentable" (vv. 22–23). God is sovereign and he makes us the way we are. Sometimes those with less equity in the eyes of the world are the most important people in the eyes of God.

The Problem with CRT

The problem in life arises when those who have no right to the equity of others, illegally take that equity that does not belong to them. They break God's law and steal. This is theft. God hates theft.

This is a major goal of CRT. It is part of the Marxist religion that has no respect for the Ten Commandments. It promotes the belief that equity should be shared equally in an unequal world, and it is the responsibility of the civil government to make it happen. It is also the responsibility of university professors and corporate leaders to make it happen. The resolution to inequity in their minds is the re-distribution of wealth (equity).

White Privilege and White Supremacy

At this point, let me say that I do think whites in America have been *privileged*. I've never personally met a white supremacist, but I think we do have to admit that whites have a lot of equity. They have inherited hundreds of years of human capital that has been handed down by their forefathers, often going all the way back to our European and Christian ancestors who came to this land. This is not white supremacy. White supremacy is a sinful attitude toward others who are not white. White supremacy is the intent to belittle or do harm to anyone not like the white man.

As I pointed out above, in general, white privilege is either gained through things like being in a biblical family, hard work, or inheritance. Those of us living today who have inherited white privilege should be thankful for the grace of God. As descendants of Adam, we did not deserve it any more than anyone else. However, this does not mean that we must institute a system that demands the relinquishment of that equity.

The Christian Faith and Privilege

It is my main contention in this book that Christianity gives privilege. I've seen this in both black and white families. Until a minority person or race (either white or black) adopts the Christian view of the home where godly fathers take responsibility for their wives and children, nothing will change. The only hope for the black individual or the black race is a return to a full-orbed Christian Faith.

The black race, as a whole, has indeed not enjoyed the privileges of the white race. The exceptions are mostly black athletes. However, if the black race adopts Christian values, then they will begin the process that will bring them the privileges that whites possess. The answer to the CRT religion is not the intervention of civil government to guarantee by legislation equity in this world, but rather the preaching of the whole counsel of God. The preaching of the gospel will not make us all the same, but it will enable others to participate in the privileges that have been enjoyed by the white race. Marxism will not accomplish this. Marxism legalizes theft. Marxism is the enemy of the gospel. It will only bring more struggle and conflict between the races. It cannot bring life and freedom.

Conclusion

I've gone back before the existence of time to demonstrate the origins of the words equality and inequity in the very character of God. The relationship between the three persons of the Trinity provides a model or paradigm for mankind. All three persons of the Trinity are equal in position, power, and eternity. However, they each have different functions. They differ in equity. There is inequity. However, there is no jealousy or covetousness. There is perfect peace in their diversity. These views must be foundational definitions as we engage in conversation today about CRT.

I've given some practical examples of how equity originates and therefore how inequity originates. I have given the reader an expanded definition of wealth. The attempt to acquire wealth lawfully is not a problem with God, and it should not be a problem with us. To mandate equity by force in a world of inequity, especially through taxation or through corporate bullying is sinful. It is Marxism. It is a form of robbery. It must be resisted. *Thus, when you hear the cry for equity from the CRT movement, think of the attempt to negate inequity by the redistribution of wealth via force.* That's the bottom line. I hope I have made it clear in this chapter.

Because the chant for equity is mostly used today in the context of races (especially white and black), we need to understand why there are different races on this earth, and what are the differences among them. We will consider this in the next chapter.

Chapter 3
Race and Nations

Are Races Real or Are They a Social Construct?

After reading a number of books on Critical Race Theory (CRT) by evangelical and reformed authors, I have become convinced that sometimes good men get it wrong. Some of the writers I respect the most are saying that the existence of distinct human races is not real. It is just a social construct.

Now, what is a social construct? It is a convention adopted by society that has no basis in objective reality. For example, Peter Pan is a social construct. We all know who he is, but he is not real. He exists in the mind for entertainment purposes. A dollar bill is a social construct. It only has value because society has given it value. In reality, it is only paper and ink.

Social constructs are usually identified with Neo-Marxist thinking. For example, Neo-Marxists say that binary sexual identification is not real. The concept of sex that separates humans into male or female is a social construct. They push the concept that, in reality, there is a multitude of sexes (they prefer the term gender). As another example, they teach that the traditional family is a social construct. The idea of a male and female parent with children is a convention created by society to oppress other legitimate families like those who have two males as parents.

I am hearing from my respected brethren that race is not a biblical term, and therefore the concept of race does not exist. At the same time, these same men will say that there is only one race, and that is the human race. The human race includes all of us because we all come from the same Adam. There is no difference between us other than the degree of melanin (pigment) in the skin.

It seems rather contradictory to me to assert that the concept of race is not real, but then to turn around and use the term race to describe all of the descendants of Adam. There are no races, but yet, there is one race?

It is true that the Bible does not use the word race in any English translation. More common terms are nation, tribe, clan, and peoples. However, the Bible does not use the term banana either, but that does not mean it is wrong to use the word banana. Historically, mankind has been divided into races. Three prominent races are whites, blacks, and Asians (with variations in-between). They have differed in more than pigmentation of the skin. They have been associated with not only the color of the skin, but with the texture of the hair, the shape of the eyes, and even in physical speed and agility. If you have ever watched a college NCAA basketball game, you will see what I mean. I don't believe that speaking this way is racist. It may be more racist to avoid reality and to say that all athletes are the same in their ability whether white or black. We need to learn to be honest.

Christians do not need to adopt the Neo-Marxist theory of race as a social construct to do battle against the CRT of Neo-Marxism. It is better to recognize the truth that distinct races do exist in objective reality, and that good and bad attributes become characteristics of races (and also nations) as a result of the religion that dominates them. This includes both black and white. Most of the average guys that I know in the pew think that this "Neo-Marxist social construct invention" is nonsensical. There is nothing to be gained by denying the obvious.

Awakenings

There have been several periods in my life that were "theological crisis moments." One was when I learned about the doctrine of justification by faith alone. My only hope is in the imputed righteousness of Christ that comes from outside of me. I have no hope in myself. Another moment was the time when I came to understand the doctrine of election. This led me to the doctrines of grace where I know that I can add nothing to my salvation — not even the act of a free-will independent of God.

One other moment was when I came to see the doctrine of the covenant in the Bible as it applies to our children and our children's children. My responsibility as a Christian father would impact generations to come. My faith was more than a personal experience. This was a major awakening!

I could easily include the change in my view regarding eschatology (study of the end times). This changed my life dramatically. I slowly cast off the dark pessimism in exchange for a future of hope. I will get into this in a later chapter.

Lastly, I had always been confused about the concept of a nation in the Bible. We all have visual images of biblical concepts. In seminary I identified the Kingdom of God with the church. As such, my idea of the Kingdom of God was a small group of God's elect gathered together as one people from various nations or races worshiping Christ. Diversity in one building was my visual image. Probably too, these Christians were waiting on the rapture or death, whichever came first.

However, after my seminary training, I did a special study on the concept of a "nation" as it was used in the Bible. I came to conclude that I had it all wrong.

The Definition of a Nation

There are three parameters in the Bible that define a nation. The first is the characteristic of a *common language*. People of the same nation speak the same language. On the day of Pentecost in the Book of Acts, we are told that there were Jews living in Jerusalem, "devout men from every nation under heaven" (Acts 2:5). The miracle of Pentecost was that the men present from a multitude of nations heard the apostles "speak in his own language" (2:6). Thus, it is clear in the Bible that a nation is defined by a common language.

Secondly, the Bible teaches that by God's providence the people of each nation have a *common border*. In the Book of Acts when the Apostle Paul was speaking on Mars Hill in Athens, he told the audience that God "made from one man every nation of mankind to live on all the face of the earth, having determined their appointed times and the boundaries of their habitation" (17:26). Thus, in defining a nation, geographical borders must be a part of that definition. Paul assumed this as part of his definition of a nation in his sermon.

Thirdly, a *common god* or religion is the third leg of three in the definition of a nation. In Psalm 96 the Psalmist says that we are to tell of "His glory to all the nations" (v. 3). We are also to tell them that "He is to be feared above all gods. For all of the gods of the peoples are idols" (vv. 4–5). This is biblical evangelism. All nations have gods and religions, and we are to call those who worship false gods to repent of their idolatry. From Baal in Palestine, to Allah in Arabia, to the God of the Bible in the Holy Roman Empire, every nation has a god from which it derives its laws and hopes for the future. This includes the present-day religion of Secular Democracy in America.

Unity and Diversity in Christ

Now, we know for certain that everyone in all the nations do descend from Adam, and we all are sinners needing a Savior. Yet, we also still exist as part of distinct races, even where different races live in the same nation (who probably have more in common than not). Jeremiah identified the Ethiopian as a man who could not change the color of his skin (12:23). Just as important as remarking on the color of his skin, the prophet noted that the man was an Ethiopian (Cushite) who probably lived south of Egypt, and who could be identified with a nation that had geographical boundaries, a separate language, and a separate religion. In the New Testament an Ethiopian eunuch became a Christian, which certainly teaches us that the gospel came as a blessing for all nations and races.

The Book of Revelation speaks of the New Jerusalem as being a dwelling place for the nations and the kings of the earth (21:24). Nations will not disappear, even in the future in the very presence of God himself. All the distinct nations along with their kings shall be one in Christ, but they will still be distinct nations

Interracial Marriage and Interracial Churches

The Bible does not forbid interracial marriages. However, I believe that interracial marriages will always be a minority sector of society.

Local churches are often a mixture of various races. In the early church in Jerusalem, many Jews who had been identified as Jews, and other Jews who had been identified as Gentiles (Grecians), were part of the same local congregation (Acts 6:1). However, even today, various races often prefer to worship with others of their own race. In the Presbyterian Church in America (PCA), there exists in the United States numerous Korean churches, and even a large number of Korean presbyteries (which consist of a multitude of churches in a common geographical area).

The Apostle Paul in the Book of Galatians says that "There is neither Jew nor Greek, there is neither slave nor free man, there is neither male nor female; for you are all one in Christ Jesus" (3:28). In Christ, we are all equal in regard to our access to the blessings that come from him, and we must all love one another with a love worthy of the love of Christ for us (Col. 3:11–14). We are to love each other as if those distinctions did not exist.

However, this does not invalidate the distinctions that Paul uses to demonstrate our equality. There still is a difference between males and females, not only physically, but in function. Females are equal to men in Christ, but they are restricted from holding office in the church. There is a difference in equity.

Just as the distinction between male and female still exists, we should not be surprised that the other distinctions would also continue to exist as well. In a world cursed by the Fall in the Garden of Eden, slavery will probably always exist in some form or other in this world. In Eph. 6:4, Paul tells Christian slaves "to be obedient to those who are your masters."

Jews will continue to exist as a distinct people until they are called to Christ through the preaching of the gospel. "For I do not want you, brethren, to be uninformed of the mystery — so that you will not be wise in your own estimation — that a partial hardening has happened to Israel until the fulness of the Gentiles has come in"

(Rom. 11:25). We have yet to see this vast conversion of the Jewish people to Christ. Even after their conversion, they will be Jewish Christians.

Realizing that a nation consists of a people (and sometimes a race) with a common language, border, and religion, this does not contradict the words of Peter where he writes to the church, "But ye are a chosen generation, a royal priesthood, a holy nation, a peculiar people; that ye should shew forth the praises of him who hath called you out of darkness into his marvelous light" (1 Pet. 2:9). Peter was speaking to the converted Jews of the New Testament as opposed to the unbelieving Jews of the Old Testament. Peter's reference to the generation of the New Testament Jews as a holy nation does not nullify the biblical definition of a nation over the timeline of history, including the modern era.

The Tower of Babel

The origin of nations can be traced back to Genesis 11 in the Bible. Those generations who lived after Noah gathered together to construct a large tower that would demonstrate their independence from God. They had already apostatized, so quickly after the Flood! God stopped this movement by creating confusing languages and disbursing the people throughout the world. Thus, here we have the beginning of nations defined both by confusing languages and geographical locations. They soon, no doubt, created their own gods and thus we have the third marker of a nation — religion.

Probably the languages were divided according to *clans* (who already existed) which created another characteristic of nations in history, an identity according to the head (the patriarch) of the clan (or tribe). God would not have created different languages for husbands and wives or for their children. God would not have broken up marriages or patriarchal families as part of his judgment (Gen. 10). These clans must have developed into what later became various nations that represented the three major races in various locations: the white Europeans, the eastern Asians, and the black Africans. The history of nations appears to bear this out. Why do the major races have distinguishing physical traits? I think the most plausible explanation is simply genetic changes over time since the Flood. Genetic mutations are quite common and could easily be a reason for the differences in races.

Balkanization in America

In history, nations have generally been identified with a specific race. America is a rather new experiment in societies, and it appears to be disintegrating rather quickly. To account for our unique status in history, we have invented a new word — ethnicity. We now use the term ethnicity to refer to various races and original nationalities that have come to comprise one nation. We have Afro-Americans, Hispanic Americans, Muslim Americans, etc.

The United States was once a Christian nation (with a common language and border), and this common religion provided a basis for the unity of the various races among us. We have changed religions (from Christianity to a Secular Democracy), and therefore we no longer have any basis for peace among us. A nation without a common religion will not long endure, just as a nation without a common geographical border or a common language will not long endure. America is being balkanized (divided) before our very eyes. From Blacks in the large cities, to Muslims in Detroit, to White Europeans in fly-over America, we are being separated into tribes. A common religion (or at least the majority religion of Christianity) has held us together, but as Christianity dies in the West,[5] America is changing rapidly.

A New Tower of Babel

After Babel the attempt to unify all the nations of the world apart from the worship of the true God should be expected to arise again, not only because of the decline of the Christian Faith, but also as a result of war and slavery. Slavery has been a part of the history of a multitude of nations since the Fall of man in the Garden.

---

[5] Pat Buchannan, *The Death of the West* (New York: St. Martin's Press).

Often, slaves would eventually become part of the enslaving nation or empire. This is especially true of America.

Since modern technology has lessened the barrier of language and geographical distance, Globalism is now a second attempt to rebuild the Tower of Babel. The common religion being pushed today, especially by American leaders, is Secular Democracy. This will fail because the only person who can unite separate nations (or races) under a common religion is Christ. Christ will begin this through the preaching of the gospel and it will end in his rule over all the nations. This will happen at the consummation of the ages. Matthew Henry's remarks on this event in his Commentary on Genesis is as pertinent today as it was when he wrote it.

> The builders departed according to their families, and the tongue they spoke, to the countries and places allotted to them. The children of men never did, nor ever will, come all together again, till the great day, when the Son of man shall sit upon the throne of his glory, and all the nations shall be gathered before him.[6]

White Privilege

Are white people in their hearts any better than black people? Or, are black people in their hearts any better than white people? Assuming the doctrine of the sinfulness of all mankind as the seed of Adam, let's look at it another way. If the roles in history were reversed and the Christian Faith had conquered Africa rather than Europe, the privilege we see today would have been the inheritance of the black man. There is no reason to think that blacks would have treated whites any better than some whites have treated blacks in the past.

White privilege can be defined as the inherent advantages possessed by a white person, especially those advantages that exist in western nations such as the United States.

It would seem rather obvious that white privilege has existed in the United States from its beginnings. White people have domi-

---

[6] Matthew Henry, *Commentary on the Book of Genesis*, see: Genesis Chapter 11.

nated the demographics of America and are prominent in her history. White people have controlled most of America's wealth, and have occupied elevated positions in education, civil government, and business. Historically, this was mostly true of white males.

All races were born into sin, and all nations have the same depravity rooted deep in their hearts. Whites are not by nature more sinful than those of any other color. We all wallow in the same mud.

A popular tendency today is to blame white privilege on the evils of the past including the appalling slavery in the South, the western expansion of white men at the expense of the Indian nations, and the malevolence of the white business tycoons. Many other malicious causes could be added to the list. There is some basis for culpability in these accusations among some of our white forefathers. However, whites are not more sinful than any other color. If the tables had been turned, and blacks had owned the plantations and whites had been subjected as slaves, the outcome would have been no different. We would be talking about black privilege today. To expect anything else is also a form of racism.

Where then does white privilege find its origin? If we admit that slavery was a contributor to white privilege, we must also consider that American history began long before the Civil War or even before Colonial America. Looking from a long-term historical perspective, we must reach back into pre-American history to understand the differences among the races.

One thing that strikes me as missing in this conversation on white privilege is the fact that mostly white men settled the original thirteen colonies, creating a culture from which came such documents as the Declaration of Independence and the United States Constitution. These white men were greatly influenced by the Christian Faith of Great Britain. Actually, American history began long before the Pilgrims. It goes back to a Christianized Europe.

This leads to the follow-up question. Why did the influence of Christianity move through Europe rather than through Africa or the Far East? The answer is the same as the response given to those who object to the doctrine of predestination. Salvation is totally by the grace of God. There is nothing in man that contributes to that salvation. Salvation depends totally on the decrees of God as they are manifested in the individual in space and time. Likewise, the same rationale can be applied to national white privilege in both Europe and America. God himself chose to spread his gospel mainly through Europe. White goodness or superiority had nothing to do with it. This prosperity was rooted in God's sovereign grace. It is also interesting to note that as Christianity today is disappearing in the traditional Western nations, it is seeing rapid growth in places like Asia, Africa, and parts of Central and South America.

American whites must not forget that God can reject a people of privilege if they squander his blessings. We find this example among the Old Testament Jews who were a privileged people. I am afraid we are seeing it in America today.

Generational Sin

The assumption today is that my generation is responsible for the sins of the past. However, children are not responsible for the sins of their fathers. The Bible clearly teaches this. The following is a quote from Ezekiel 18:19–20:

> Yet you say, "Why should the son not bear the punishment for the father's iniquity?" When the son has practiced justice and righteousness and has observed all my statutes and done them, he shall surely live. The person who sins will die. The son will not bear the punishment for the father's iniquity, nor will the father bear the punishment for the son's iniquity; the righteousness of the righteous will be upon himself, and the wickedness of the wicked will be upon him.

My ancestors have been in America since the late 1600s, but none of them ever owned any slaves. Some fought for the South in the Civil War, but they were not fighting for slavery but were fighting for States' rights. My great-grandfather was fighting against the intrusion of the federal government into the commonwealth of Virginia. My ancestors who fought in the Civil War really had no interest in slavery. Regardless, even if I had ancestors who were ungodly slave-owners, according to the Scriptures, I could not be held responsible for their sins.

Some nations consist of mainly one race, and other nations consist of various races. Oftentimes, what can be said of a nation can also be said of a race, and what can be said of a race can be said of a nation. One of the interesting things I have learned in studying the Bible is how the Apostle Paul viewed the Cretans in the Bible. He saw them as a corporate body. He dealt with them as a nation, not just as individuals. He derided them as lazy gluttons. Being a Jew, was Paul a racist? Absolutely not! Let's look at this in more detail as I pose and answer a few questions. The following is an article I wrote some years ago in the *Aquila Report*, and I thought it might be beneficial for the readers of this book.

Was the Apostle Paul a Racist?

By today's definition of racism, the Apostle Paul could easily be identified as a racist or a Jewish Nationalist. The words of Paul that could lend credence to his racism were penned by him in Titus 1:12. There he affirms the words of the Grecian poet (Epimenides) who said that the Cretans (who resided on the island of Crete in the Mediterranean Sea), viewed as a people or nation, were "always liars, evil beasts, lazy gluttons." As Cretans were converted to Christ, Paul tells Titus that he should expect to see this indwelling sin in these people, and he will need to "reprove them severely" (v. 13) in aiding them in their sanctification because this was such a dominant trait in their particular ethnic group.

Paul writes as a Jew to Gentiles. The Cretans had a propensity as a people to lie, to prey on others, and to be lazy. They would rather eat than work. John Gill says, in his commentary written in the 18th century on the book of Titus:

> It was a sin they were addicted to; some countries are disting-
> uished by their vices; some for pride; some for levity, vanity, and
> inconstancy; some for boasting and bragging; some for covet-
> ousness; some for idleness; some for effeminacy; some for hypo-

crisy and deceit; and others, as the Cretans, it seems for lying; this was their national sin.[7]

Making such a statement as Paul did in the Book of Titus would be considered in our modern culture as being insensitive to people "not like us." To identify a body of people who are dominated by a particular sin surely seems sinful itself. To most Christians and many clergymen in the modern church, it smacks of racism. American clergymen who are unable to think outside of the paradigm of individualism, are thus unable to recognize national traits — unless it is the guilt of being a white man. However, we are not just individuals. We all identify with a nation, with a race, and even with a particular family. We all have surnames. We all identify with corporate bodies. Just listen to a typical evangelical sermon on Psalm 2 about the nations who roar against God, and watch how quickly it can become a Psalm on individual piety rather than the necessity of all the kings of the earth bowing before the Holy God. In an attempt to balance the modern drift toward the formation of unbiblical concepts (even in evangelical circles), I think a good instructive method here is simply to ask a series of questions.

Question: What is racism?

Answer: All men are created in the image of God and to despise or hate a man simply because he is of a different race or nation is racism. To treat persons unfairly because of their race or nationality is sinful. To distinguish various qualities (good and bad) among the various races or nations is not racism.

Question: What are some of the good distinguishable qualities of the various nations?

Answer: Germans have been known for their musical abilities (Bach, Beethoven, Brahms, etc.). The British seemed to have dominated literature (Chaucer, Shakespeare, Dickens, etc.). America has been known for technological innovation.

Question: What are some of the bad distinguishable qualities of various nations?

---

[7] John Gill, *Commentary on the Book of Titus,* see Titus 1.

Answer: If you had lived through World War II, then at that time, the Germans would have been identified as arrogant and haughty. Today, among black Americans, nearly 80% of the children are born outside of wedlock. American Whites are trailing but catching up. Whites in the United States, who control much of the wealth, are mostly dominated by Darwinian anthropology and are thus existential materialists.

Question: What is the most prominent reason that the races or nationalities are different?

Answer: The most prominent contributor to the difference between the races is religion, not color or physical characteristics. For example, biblical Christianity (not the liberal type) makes a nation different. Biblical Christianity makes people oriented toward the nuclear family which consists of a father and mother, upholds contracts, protects life, holds a high work ethic, values education, and results in the worship of the Triune God.

Question: Is it then racist to distinguish certain characteristics among races and nations?

Answer: No, there are real differences between the nations and races, and acknowledging those differences can be profitable for all of us. God created a world of diversity among the races and nations (and among individuals), and we should rejoice in that. Sin created ethnic vices that capture people as a whole. What captures the nations will capture most individuals in that nation. When a false religion (which includes Secular Humanism) captures a nation or race, it spreads sinful traits that can be overcome only by the gospel.

Like the Apostle Paul, we should recognize that those traits do exist among both nations and races, and we should offer both individuals and nations (and races) the only hope possible, which is in Christ alone. There is nothing racist in doing that.

Buying and Selling Slaves

Dr. Voddie Bachman, a black minister, states in his Book *Fault-lines*[8] that probably black slaves were the result of black people in Africa capturing other black men and turning them into slaves. White men did not enter the bushes of Africa to capture the black man. Black men captured the black man and sold him as slaves to White Europeans, and to other nations.

In an article titled *Unspoken Reality – Black Slaveholders Prior to the Civil War*[9], the authors point out that American slaveholders prior to the Civil War were both Black and White (and also Indian). There were numerous Black slaveholders in the South. Five Native American Tribes, i.e., Cherokee, Chickasaw, Choctaw, Creek, and Seminole held thousands of black slaves.

As the blacks came into America as slaves, they tended to adopt the religion of the slave-owners. They mostly became Christians. However, Black Christianity after the Civil War could not keep their fathers in the home. In many ways Black Christianity failed the Black Race. This created a vacuum. Islam became a substitute at one time and created the Black Muslim movement. Today, CRT threatens to fill that vacuum.

Indeed, many whites who are descendants of slave-owners are beginning to recognize the guilt of many of their forefathers. Some progress has been made here. I think sympathy is appropriate. However, the white-guilt narrative has its limits. As a white man today, I can be sympathetic to the plight of blacks both in history and in the modern day, but this does not mean I must be held responsible for their predicament.

---

[8] Voddie Baucham, *Fault Lines*, 71.

[9] *Abstract* of Yuliya Tikhomirova and Lucia Desir, "Unspoken *Reality: Black Slaveholders Prior to the Civil War.*" Mercy College, *Undergraduate Research Journal for the Human Sciences* (kon.org). https://www.kon.org/urc/v4/ tik ho mirova.html

Conclusion

We are all descendants of Adam and in that sense, we are all equal. However, races and nations often have different gifts and abilities. Diversity extends beyond the individual to families, races, and nations. Calling the concept of race a social construct is not going to solve any problems.

America is an example of white men from Christian Europe who settled this country, and brought the fruit of the Christian Faith with them. They transported equity with them. They created more equity by living out the Christian Faith. When blacks came to America, they did not bring this same equity with them, and the result was slavery. Blacks have made considerable progress over the years toward reaching the equity of the white race. We can all rejoice in this.

Christianity took seed in Europe but not in Africa. Even though blacks tended to adopt Christianity in America, it did not have the impact on their homes and families as it has on whites. Black Christianity failed to capture the hearts of the black fathers. The black family was nearly destroyed, and therefore, the black race has continued to suffer. This is the major culprit that contributed to the racial inequity that still exists in our society today. All the other panaceas like affirmative action, quotas based on numbers and not merit, legislation, and CRT will fail the black race. They will only result in more tension between the races.

Neo-Marxism is seeking to exploit those tensions for the sake of establishing itself as the new religion of America. Both blacks and whites are being deceived. Neo-Marxism seeks peace via theft. Christianity seeks peace via the cross. It's important to understand the origins and nature of Neo-Marxism. We shall look at its origins and character in the next chapter.

Chapter 4
Neo-Marxism

A New Religion

As I mentioned in Chapter One, the root of all religious movements was in the Garden of Eden. It was there that the truth of God's Word was doubted, and Adam and Eve wanted to be equal with God. They were not content with simply being creatures made in the image of God (inequity). They demanded *equity*. Because of their sin, we are all born into sin. God the Father sent his Son to die for the world so that we might be put back into a right relationship with God. Christians know their place in this life. God is the Creator and we are the creatures.

Therefore, from the view of biblical Christianity, there are only two religions – Christianity and everything else. One of the manifestations of that "everything else" is what has been called Marxism.

Karl Marx

Karl Marx, the father of Marxism, was Born in Trier, Prussia (now Germany), on May 5, 1818. Marx was the son of a successful Jewish lawyer who converted to Lutheranism before Marx's birth. Marx was an atheist all of his adult life. He studied law in Bonn and Berlin. In Berlin he became involved with radical movements of the day at a young age through a group called Young Hegelians. Marx received his doctorate from the University of Jena in 1841. His beliefs prevented him from securing a teaching position, so instead, he took a job as a journalist and later became the editor of a liberal newspaper in Cologne, Germany.

After living in Prussia, Marx lived in France for some time, and that is where he met his lifelong friend Friedrich Engels. He was expelled from France in 1849 and then lived for a brief period in Belgium before moving to London, England, where he spent the rest of his life.

Marx, in conjunction with Fredrick Engels, published *The Communist Manifesto* in 1848; later in life, he wrote *Das Kapital*. The first volume of the latter book was published in Berlin in 1867; the second and third volumes were published posthumously in 1885 and 1894. The influence of Karl Marx in history cannot be underestimated. His writings have had a major impact in history, possibly only rivaled by the Bible itself.

Marx died of bronchitis and pleurisy in London on March 14, 1883. The Tomb of Karl Marx stands in the Eastern Cemetery of Highgate Cemetery, in North London, England.

Marxism

Marxism always comes out of a cultural context that is generally defined by class struggles (whether real or perceived). In regard to Karl Marx, his particular target was what he perceived as the dominance of one particular economic class over another. It is true that very often wealth accumulates in the hands of a few who are extravagant and have great hostility toward the poor. This has been true of history down through the ages.

Great wealth-barons have spotted the landscape of America, but they helped in the formation of the Middle Class by creating jobs for the working man. America over the last century can be described as a nation with a large Middle Class. People in the Middle Class usually have a job where they make a livable wage. They are able to buy a home. They generally have access to quality medical care. They take vacations, and sometimes send their children off to college. Marxism will usually have very little opportunity to take root in a nation with a large Middle Class. America still has a large Middle Class; however, a new form of Marxism is targeting this Middle Class.

The older views of Marxism divided society into the *haves* and *have-nots*. A Marxist believes that those who have a great deal of wealth gained it through the oppression of the poor. This original view of Marx has been called Classical Marxism. Marx identified the haves as the *bourgeois* and the have-nots as the *proletariat*. The bourgeois were the merchants, landowners and lawyers (the upper class), and the proletariat were the laborers (the working class). Since, in the mind of Marx, life is a constant economic war, and the working class does not share in the wealth of the merchants, the only way to level the classes is by taking from the rich and giving to the poor.

According to Classical Marxism, in order to achieve this utopia on earth, there must be a transfer of wealth and this can only be accomplished through a revolution with guns and bloodshed. All property must be redistributed in the name of equality, and this by force. Ultimately, this will make everyone equal and everyone will be happy being equal. Inequity must be ended! This religion must not be merely a theory in a textbook, but it must be put into action.

And it was. Beginning with Russia in 1917 in the Bolshevik Revolution, millions were killed and their property was redistributed. It eventually spread to many other nations, including China, North Korea, Cuba, and parts of South America. It is estimated that over 100 million people have died in the 20th century as a result of the spread of Marxism. This is one reason why we must take even Neo-Marxism very seriously.

Marxism had one grave error embedded in its call for the redistribution of wealth. Instead of creating a utopia of equality, it became a tyranny of a few rich over a multitude of the poor. Marxism always creates a small wealthy class that despises the poor. Ironically, it produces what it claims to hate. Everyone (except the few in charge who live extravagantly) is equal. Equally poor!

Neo-Marxism and Cultural Marxism

Since early Marxism ended in catastrophe, later in the early 20th century others who were sympathetic to Marxism developed a new plan to implement the basic ideas of Marx. I call it Neo-Marxism.

This movement originated in Frankfurt, Germany, beginning with people with names like Antonio Gramsci, George Lukas, and Max Horkheimer. It spread to America when Herbert Marcuse came to teach at Columbia University in New York City (then considered a Teacher's College). German-born Marcuse also taught at Harvard and Brandeis Universities. Eventually, Neo-Marxism would spread and capture most of the universities in America. It would later be propagated by men like John Dewey. Mark Levin details this in his book *American Marxism*.[10] For Neo-Marxism to succeed there has to be a change in both the method of capturing a nation, and also a change in the scope of the definition of the class struggle.

A Change in Method

One of the ultimate goals for these men was still the redistribution of wealth (equity) in the name of equality, but they realized that the method needed to change. Instead of a militant revolution with guns and bloodshed, the method of changing the religion of nations must be slow and deliberate. It must be a bloodless coup. It must happen over time (decades) by infiltrating the cultural structures in the nations themselves, beginning with the universities. From the universities, since they have so much influence over all the other structures of society, it would flow to the media, to the civil government, the public schools, the military, sports, and even to the church.

Most Middle-Class Americans did not know it, but for almost a century now they have been sending their children off to college to become Neo-Marxists. They have been paying for these schools through their taxes. Also, it's amazing how many evangelical and reformed seminaries in America have been infiltrated by this new religion.[11] And, remember, what comes to the seminaries, eventually comes to the local church. Cultural Marxists call this entire process *the long march through the institutions*.

The method is also called incrementalism. Everything happens slowly over a long period of time in small and unnoticeable increments. It's a little like the proverbial frog in a pot of boiling water. He does not know the danger he is in until it is too late. A few bold prophets point out the danger, but they are considered delusional.

---

[10] Mark Levin, *American Marxism* (New York: Threshold, 2021).

[11] See: Jon Harris, *Christianity and Social Justice: Religions in Conflict* (Ann Arbor, Mich: Reformation Zion, 2021). www.reformationzion.com.

To accomplish this slow march in order to change the religion of America, there needed to be a change in the mindset of the American people. Most Americans do not consider themselves as victims, so a bloody war would not be possible. Doug Enick describes this obstacle to the "guns and guts" method by the American people in his book *Social Justice and its Dangers*:

> The reason the masses in Western nations haven't risen up in violent revolution against their unjust capitalists oppressors is because the cultural forces in those nations have conditioned them to think they're not oppressed, and that if they were oppressed, violent revolution would be a morally wrong way to address it.[12]

In other words, a militant revolution would not work in America. Americans, in general, do not think of themselves as being oppressed. Minority Americans believe that the road to the Middle Class and beyond is still open. Therefore, division within the nation must be created, and the road to this goal must advance gradually by capturing the institutions of America over time. While Neo-Marxist were planning for the future, Christians were waiting for the rapture (see the next chapter).

Neo-Marxists have been very fruitful. Anyone who does not agree with their principles, especially as it expresses itself in the CRT movement, is now called a White Supremacist. He is considered a racist. Division in America is growing at a dramatic pace.

A Change in Scope

Also, the scope of equality needed to change from Classical Marxism that focused only on economic relations between the classes. There needed to be changes made in the other areas of life where there are differences among people. For example, the difference between male and female needed to be attacked. The difference between white and black needed to be dismantled. Traditional differences in our culture that came from Christianity needed to be

---

[12] Doug Enick, *Social Justice and Its Dangers* (Coulterville, Calif.: Center for Cultural Leadership, 2019), 13.

rejected. This included the traditional view of marriage, homo-sexuality, and transgenderism. The whole Christian culture, which had been based on Christian principles, needed to be *canceled*.

Just like in the Book of Acts, as Christianity turned the world upside-down, Neo-Marxists believe the world needs to be turned up-side down again, only this time by a new religion. Preaching points would begin in the university classroom and spread to the media and civil government. The term for this new twist on the old Classical Marxism was called Cultural Marxism (or Neo-Marxism). The entire culture needed to be changed. There needed to be what has been called a *Great Reset*. Since the old culture was based on the Christian Faith, the institutions that identified with Christendom must be infiltrated, and changed.

Incremental Success

The Neo-Marxists have been very successful up to this point. They have indeed captured the universities. Almost every university and college in American now has a Department of Diversity. If a professor at almost any university in the States objects to CRT, he will most likely be fired. Many already have been terminated.

The most critical decision of the Supreme Court in recent years was *Obergefell v. Hodges* in 2015. It made homosexual marriage legal in all 50 states. Sodomy became a constitutional right. Just 30 years before this decision, homosexual marriage was unthinkable in the minds of most Americans. Mark this up as another victory for Neo-Marxism. It happened over time while most Americans slept.

I remember making a trip to the State Capitol of Tennessee to contest the *Obergefell* ruling becoming law in my State. The Ten-nessee State Constitution forbids marriage by two persons of the same sex. The Constitution had recently been updated by a majority vote of more than 80% of the citizens of the State to clearly state that marriage could only be between those of the opposite sex. I failed to convince the legislative committee who considered this Supreme Court Decision (I did, by God's grace, change the mind of one legislator).

As I reminded the legislators that homosexual marriage was illegal in the State of Tennessee, they responded with two justifications to ignore this statute. One was that the decision of the Supreme Court overruled State Constitutions. The other was that if the State did not comply with the decision of the U. S. Supreme Court, the State would lose its funding from the Federal Government. So, the Constitution of the State of Tennessee is now null and void. Mark up another big win here for Neo-Marxism.

The Family and Neo-Marxist Strategy

One major strategy of Neo-Marxism is to destroy the nuclear family. This is done in a number of ways. First, target the Christian stereotypes of responsible fatherhood in the home, where a man both provides financially for his family and protects his home against dangerous enemies. Create new stereotypes of "men in skirts" on the one hand, or "toxic masculinity" on the other hand. Make the fictitious character *Superman* bisexual. Reduce the marriage rates and increase the divorce rates. Decry corporal punishment as child-abuse. Create gender confusion beginning with young children where they don't know if they are really girls or boys. Flood the media market with nudity, pornography, adultery, and fornication. Feed the nation with dangerous drugs that will be purchased by people living in misery. Create chaos in society so that the people will cry out for someone to rule over them, and that person will probably be a Neo-Marxist.

Conclusion

As Christianity dies in the West (see ch. 6), it is being replaced by Neo-Marxism (also called Cultural Marxism). Sadly, much of the church is joining forces with this new religion (although they keep their Christian terminology and rituals). If the church is not joining in with this movement, then they are simply remaining quiet about it. I am afraid this is our guilty silence while this cancer spreads rather quickly now.

In my mind, the church's response to Neo-Marxism can be compared to a man inside a house trying to determine what color to paint the living room while a fire rages outside of his front door. The homeowners just ignore the fire. I think the church is exactly like this. It is clueless. It cannot see that its house is about to be burned to the ground. The Church is mostly dominated today by 1) R2K Theology, 2) Christian Pietism, and 3) Escapism. I shall describe each of these in the next chapter. These three things have made the church irrelevant to the culture in which we live. The church has ceased to be the salt of the earth.

Chapter 5
The Plight of the Modern Evangelical Church

A Definition of The Kingdom of God

A kingdom includes everything over which a king reigns. In the Old Testament the word kingdom was used to describe the extensive realms of various kings from those like the Kingdom of Sihon to the Kingdom of Og, and likewise to the Kingdom of David. Just like the word *nation*, of which the meaning did not change from the Old Testament to the New Testament (see ch. 3), neither does the word *kingdom* change from the Old to the New.

The Kingdom of God describes the realm over which God rules. God rules over the hearts of his people. His Kingdom is indeed internal. However, God's Kingdom is also external. For instance, he rules over creation. He also rules over his church. The Kingdom is both inside of the heart and outside of the heart. Beginning from the heart, our hope is to see God's Kingdom expand to encapsulate all of culture.

Thus, the Kingdom of God is like any other kingdom. It exists wherever the Sovereign rules. When Jesus ascended to heaven, he declared that "all power has been given unto me in heaven and on earth" (Matt. 28:18). Therefore, we have the source of power to accomplish his will on earth. Jesus also told his followers to disciple the nations. "Go therefore and make disciples of all the nations, baptizing them in the name of the Father and the Son and the Holy Spirit, teaching them to observe all that I commanded you; and lo, I am with you always, even to the end of the age" (vv. 19–20). Remember my basic definition of a nation. It is defined by three characteristics. It consists of people who have a common border, a common language, and a common religion. The goal of the gospel is to capture all the nations on the earth and teach them to obey all that the Scriptures teach.

The Great Commission (Matt. 28:16–20) is the means to fulfill and expand the Creation Mandate where God told Adam and Eve to "Be fruitful and multiply, and fill the earth, and subdue it; and rule over the fish of the sea, and the birds of the sky, and over every living thing that moves on the face of the earth" (Gen. 1:28). The Apostle Paul speaks of the ultimate success of Christ on earth before his Second Coming when he says "then comes the end, when He hands over the kingdom to the God and Father, when He has abolished all rule and all authority and power. He must reign until He has put all His enemies under His feet. The last enemy that will be abolished is death" (1 Cor. 15:24–25).

I just mentioned (at the end of ch. 4) three dominating tenets that have captured the church, and hindered the accomplishment of the Great Commission. They include (1) R2K Theology, (2) Christian Pietism, and (3) Escapism. These three overlap each other, but I will deal with each one separately.

1. Radical Two-Kingdom Theology (R2K)

One of the most ominous dangers that the modern evangelical church must confront is the doctrine of Radical Two-Kingdom (R2K) Theology. There is one sense in which there are two kingdoms in the Bible — the Kingdom of God and the Kingdom of Satan. However, even though Satan is still alive and doing damage, yet his power was crushed at the cross of Christ. When I speak of R2K, I am speaking of those who divide the world into two kingdoms that consist of the church and the civil magistrate. Again, there is a sense in which the church and the civil magistrate are not the same. They each have separate functions in this world. The Church administers the sacraments, and the State administers the sword.

What then makes this separation of Church and State radical (thus Radical Two Kingdom)? The Bible teaches that Jesus is King over both the church and the state, and thus his law must be the basis for everything in both realms. If Christ is not King over all, then he is not King at all.

Jesus said to the Pharisees that they were to "render to Caesar the things that are Caesar's; and to God the things that are God's"

(Matt. 22:21). The topic of conversation was the poll tax. Indeed, we are to pay our taxes to the State and our tithes to the Church. However, we should not take this text beyond its context. We must not forget the basic assumption of the entirety of Scripture that both the Church and Caesar belong to God. God is sovereign over each, and both must recognize him as King. Romans 13:4 tells us that the civil magistrate is a minister (deacon) of God. He is no more independent of God than are the fish that swim in the sea.

Those who promote R2K restrict the kingship of Christ to the Church, and promote the idea that the State should be ruled by natural law (whatever that is). This is a radical separation of Church and State, thus the term R2K.

When R2K followers read the New Testament, they see the legitimate separation of Church and State, but they do not see the right of Christ to rule over both Church and State. You can legitimately separate Church and State, but you can't separate Church and Religion. Every State will adopt a national religion that determines the dominant law that will rule over the people. The source of law in any nation is the god of that nation.

R2K and Spirituality. R2K proponents consider the Old Testament a theocracy where God rules both Church and State. The Church is spiritual, and the State is earthly. They push the idea that in the New Testament the rule of God is totally spiritual. By spiritual they are referring to the hearts of men as opposed to the physical world. God rules in the hearts of men, in the elect only, and the ultimate goal of life is to escape this world and go to heaven (see below). What happens in the world outside of the Church is not our concern. What happens to our children in the future is not really our concern (although they are inconsistent here). We watch the world decay and pray that the coming of Christ will be soon. This is the basic paradigm or model for most modern Christians.

However, the word "spiritual" as used in the New Testament refers to the work of the Holy Spirit. Wherever you find the Holy Spirit working, there you find *spirituality*. Of course, this includes the hearts of Christians and the visible church, but it extends beyond that to every facet of life. The entire world belongs to Christ and the goal of the Holy Spirit is to extend the rule of Christ to every institution on earth, including civil government, education, medicine, law, the arts, etc. According to the Great Commission, Christ came to capture the nations of the world through the gospel, and Christ would have us use the pattern found in Old Testament Israel to be the model for modern Christian nations. Let me explain this further.

The Right Paradigm. I will propose a question here. Is the New Testament the absolute paradigm of what the kingdom of God looks like for all generations? The New Testament is new in the sense that it is better. Christ replaces all the sacrifices of the Old Testament. The gospel is now to be preached to the Gentiles (all the nations). The Holy Spirit is outpoured. But does the greatness of the New Covenant nullify the model of Old Testament Israel as the example of what a Christian nation would look like? My answer is No. It is interesting that when King David speaks of studying the law of God day and night, he was talking about the first five books of the Bible. That was the only Law he had that would enable him to fulfill his duty to be a good ruler of the nation of Israel. He spent a great amount of time studying what we call the case-laws of the Pentateuch (the first five books of Moses). Modern leaders would do well to do the same.

The New Testament was written in the context of a church that was in seed form. It was a persecuted church living with the hatred of both Jews and Romans. It was never intended to be the norm for every generation. It is my thesis that the theocracy of Israel *in principle* provides a paradigm for Christians today as we seek to bring the Kingdom of God into fullness, and as we pray to see God's will be done on earth as it is in heaven. Some generations will have to endure difficult persecution, but not all. Christians in America have enjoyed the blessings of a Christian nation for over two hundred years without persecution, and in many ways, we have followed the model of Old Testament Israel.

Would you rather be ruled in society by a loving Christ who calls civil magistrates to administer his law and grace, or would you rather be ruled by lawless men who have no regard for the God of the Bible? I would hope that the answer to that question is rather easy for you.

Our Citizenship is in Heaven. One favorite passage of the "Two-Kingdom" proponents is the quote from Philippians 3:20 where Paul says that "our citizenship is in heaven." From this text, there often arises a retreat from the responsibility to apply the law of God to all areas of life like the arts and the sciences. These are considered worldly concerns. We are told that we must be heavenly-minded because our citizenship is in heaven. Theology is limited to "spiritual issues." Christian Theology has become irrelevant to issues outside of the church. This makes it nearly impossible to challenge Neo-Marxism or CRT.

In the secular, political realm of our day, there seem to be two choices for a model nation — either progressive humanism or conservative humanism (Democrat or Republican). Christianity has been relegated to just another irrelevant "pie-in-the-sky" religion partly because Christians themselves believe that their citizenship is in heaven, and they are waiting to escape this world. As such, they have almost nothing to say about the issues of the world in which we live. It's time to debunk this myth!

We have created our own "safe space" in the church building where what is said on Sunday has little to do with what is going on in the world around us. The irony I find from attending various churches is that I have found that the political issues of the day will definitely be discussed in the church — in the foyer after the Worship Service!

What Is Citizenship? In Philippians 3:20, the King James Version translates the word "citizenship" as the word "conversation." The word "conversation" is right out of antiquity, and it means "our manner of life." Our manner of life in this world results from that which is in heaven. This is all that Paul is saying, and nothing more. The Greek word translated "citizenship" is derived from *polis* which means "city." The NASB in the margin translates it as "commonwealth." The "commonwealth of heaven" is not a relationship with another world that facilitates our escape from responsibility to apply the law of God to all areas of life in this world. It is the place that is the source of our character and deeds as Christians living here on this earth where we have a duty to extend the Kingdom of God far and wide.

The point is that heaven is the place from which we get our identity. Our lives as we live in this world reflect the character of heaven and the Christ who is in heaven. Heaven defines our rights and privileges as we live on earth. Those privileges come from God.

As we enter daily into our places of work, into our homes, and even into our churches, heaven goes with us. As an American citizen goes to Europe, his citizenship goes with him. If he is a businessman who owns a company in France, then he will be responsible to make sure the business in France is profitable. He has work to do in another country. Yet, regarding his identity, he still remains an American citizen with all the rights and privileges thereof. If he is in danger, then he can expect his homeland to come to his rescue (at least before the debacle exit in Afghanistan).

2. Christian Pietism

The antithesis (tension) in Christianity is not between the body and the spirit. It is between sin and righteousness. I am afraid that the old conflict in Greek-dualism has had too much influence on our modern theology. It teaches that the body is evil and the spirit is good. This is contrary to the Scriptures. For example, Abraham was a stranger in a foreign land, not because he was in a physical body, but because he was in a land full of idolatry. Abraham was looking for a city whose builder and maker is God, a city void of idolatry. He died without seeing that city, but a partial realization of that city would come later in the creation of Jerusalem. It will come yet in its perfection when the New Jerusalem comes "down out of heaven from God" (Rev. 21:2).

This is not to deny the effect of sin on our physical bodies and the hope that our sick and dying bodies will be transformed someday that we might live on a new earth in peace and in good health (2 Pet. 3:13) — and in the presence of Christ. Anyone with a serious or chronic illness must maintain this hope. Anyone facing death must maintain this hope. "To live is Christ and to die is gain" (Phil. 1:21).

We are strangers here on earth because it is full of idolatry, not because we are in the body and our citizenship is in heaven. In the future we will be in a new body on a new earth. Heaven is a holding place until our spirits and our bodies are reunited on Resurrection Day. Our goal while we now have life on this earth is to preach the gospel and pray that God's will shall be done on earth as it is in heaven (Matt. 6:10). The source or our strength in advancing the Kingdom of God is "not of this world" (John 18:36). We don't fight with swords, but rather with the truth and the power of the Holy Spirit. Let us reconsider this pietist misunderstanding of our citizenship being in heaven, and transform our minds to do the Lord's will here on earth in every area of life (Rom. 12:2). It is a necessary weapon in order to battle against Neo-Marxism.

Christian Pietism and the Death of American Christendom. Since the conversion of Constantine and the later events surrounding the Reformation, the West has been identified as Christian. This includes continental Europe, the British Isles, and America. The influence of Christianity was strong in all spheres of life including the arts, science, economics, family life, and civil government.

As an example of this attitude, Martin Bucer, during the Protestant Reformation, wrote a Book (*The Kingdom of Christ*), and asked that it be given to King Edward VI of England so that he might consider how to structure both the Church and society after the principles of God's word. The Christian Faith was to be the rule of faith and practice in all of life, from agriculture, law, education, and in all the other institutions on earth. You would be hard-pressed to find that kind of faith today. Although the West was far from perfect, the Bible had a consequential impact on all of life. This has traditionally been called Christendom. But everything has changed. We are no longer a Christian nation, and most preachers that I meet despise the word Christendom.

How did this decline happen so quickly? Consider two words — Christian Pietism! Christian Pietism is not the same thing as Christian Piety. Christian Piety is rooted in the fear of God from the heart, and a commitment to the expansion of God's Kingdom on earth through worship, evangelism and discipleship. It certainly includes the examination of our hearts so that we might not sin against God and we might trust in Christ for the forgiveness of our sin. However, the Kingdom of God is the arena wherever God rules, whether it be in the church, in the family, in the board room, or in the town hall.

On the other hand, Christian Pietism restricts God's rule to the heart. It identifies the kingdom with the church. It is motivated by a martyr-motif (see below), and believes that rulers outside the church are only obligated to rule by some ethereal definition of "natural law." It is salt without its savor.

A few characteristics of Christian Pietism can be identified by the following *misconceptions*.

1. *Christianity is a heart-religion*. Indeed, all issues flow from the heart, but the heart is not the ultimate locale of the fullness of the Kingdom of God. The Kingdom of God begins in the heart but it permeates every area of life.

2. *Worship is our primary responsibility*. Worship is indeed very important. It is critical! Being part of a Church is so important that our forefathers believed that ordinarily there is no salvation outside of the visible church. However, the first commandment given to man by God was to multiply and subdue the earth (the earth he had just created). We are to work six days and to worship (and rest) one.

3. *Soul-winning defines the purpose of the church*. Soul-winning is a means to an end but not the end itself. In the Great Commission, following baptism, we are commanded to disciple the nations and teach them to obey the laws of God.

4. *We must not resist the civil magistrate*. In Romans 13: 1-7, we are told to be in submission to rulers since they are ordained by God. This text clearly teaches that those civil rulers are ministers of God, and therefore we are to hold them responsible to administer God's law. Our patriot American forefathers understood the moral and legal responsibility of kings to their subjects. However, if the civil

magistrate becomes a tyrant, then it is the responsibility of a lesser civil magistrate to interpose himself between the tyranny of the higher magistrate and the Christian freedom of the people. This was the basis for the American Revolution against England. If the King becomes a godless tyrant, he forfeits his right to rule.[13]

5. *The martyr-motif is normative for the Christian life.* The New Testament church in seed form as it expanded in the culture of pagan Rome was greatly persecuted, and this has been made normative for all generations. We ignore the fact that the civil government of Old Covenant Israel provides a pattern for a Christian nation where the laws of the Christian faith provide for peace, godly justice, and mercy for all men. That is a fact. But martyrdom does not come to every generation. Some will be called to be leaders.

After the Protestant Reformation, Pietism became a strong force in the church in Germany. Pietism provides a fertile ground for the advancement of national totalitarianism. I believe the Nazi Party took advantage of this mindset in Germany during the rise of Hitler. The Nazi Party Platform of 1920 said:

We demand the freedom of all religious confessions in the state, in so far as they do not jeopardize the state's existence or conflict with the manners and the moral sentiments of the German race.[14]

The Nazi Party in the name of the people stealthily usurped the authority of God. Only the Party could define the ultimate morality of the German people. The churches could hold to their confessions, but only in so far as they did not interfere with advancement of the Third Reich. Adolf Hitler was the author of the Nazi Party Platform.

---

[13] Matthew Trewhella, *The Doctrine of the Lesser Magistrate: A Proper Resistance to the Tyranny and a Repudiation of Unlimited Obedience to Civil Government* (North Charleston, S.C.: CreateSpace, 2013).

[14] 1920 Nazi Platform, Article 24, Holocaust Museum. See: ushmm.org/content/en/article/nazi-party-platform

3. Escapism

Escapism has captured the American evangelical church including both the baptistic culture, and many amillennial Presbyterian Churches. Their kingdom of God is spiritual and their ultimate hope is to escape from life on this earth where the devil is wreaking havoc. The future here on earth is dark and dim. Of course, the church must continue to be a mission-minded people in order to gather in the remainder of God's elect, but the Kingdom of God, in their view, on this earth will ultimately fail.

In my opinion, these Christians just need to be more consistent and 1) discourage people from having children, and 2) engage the culture for one purpose only — to increase persecution and therefore hasten the rapture or the second coming. This is what I hear many Christians saying.

It is true that each individual will be on this earth for only a short time and then we "fly away" (Psa. 90:10). The Psalmist makes this clear in Psalm 103 where he says, "As for man, his days are like the grass; as a flower of the field, so he flourishes. When the wind has passed over it, it is no more, and its place acknowledges it no longer" (vv.15–16).

However, there is something very important that is always missing among Escape Theology proponents. What is missing? Our children and our children's children! In other words what is missing in Escape Theology is the covenant, the responsibility to our progeny. The Psalmist in the same Psalm 103 goes on to say, "But the lovingkindness of the Lord is from everlasting to everlasting on those who fear Him, and His righteousness to children's children, to those who keep his covenant and remember his precepts to do them" (vv. 17–18). Notice that the desire to go to heaven does not nullify the responsibility we have to our children's children.

Where is the Church When You Need Her? While Neo-Marxism and CRT rage across the landscape of America, the Church is silent. In some cases, the Church has adopted a Neo-Marxist framework into her own theology. This is a grave disappointment! In the heat of the battle against a religion seeking to destroy her, the Church seems impotent.

A few bold and capable men have written about the dangers of Neo-Marxism (Cultural Marxism). There are a few soldiers leading the charge against this false religion. These include names like Harris, Baucham, DeMar, Boot, and Sandlin, just to name a few. However, the conservative American Church, in general, appears to be in hiding. It's not what is being said in the American pulpit that bothers me. It is what is being left unsaid.

Selective Orthodoxy. Since the pastor in the typical church is a product of the seminary where he attended, I think the whole problem goes back to the seminaries. I certainly appreciate all that I learned in seminary. However, speaking for myself, I soon learned after graduating from seminary that *orthodoxy, as defined by the seminary, tends to be selective.* What was in the curriculum and what was recommended reading was excellent. What was absent from the curriculum and what was absent from recommended reading was disheartening.

For example, today I doubt that there are any classes in seminary on the topic of Neo-Marxism. In a sense, the seminary by avoiding such topics has declared these topics to be unimportant (and maybe irrelevant). Their students make the same assumption, oftentimes out of respect for their professors, and they seldom reach beyond what the seminary has declared as being the scope of orthodox theology. Maybe seminaries consider such topics as too political? Maybe they believe that it is a dangerous mixture of church and state? Maybe some professors are closet Neo-Marxists? Maybe some are open Neo-Marxists, and they are tolerated to keep the peace? Then too, maybe the supporters of the seminary would stop giving money to the school if the seminary started dealing with "political issues?" The point is that preachers are a reflection of what they learned in seminary. They seldom venture beyond the cubicle of restricted orthodoxy as defined by their seminary.

A Good Shepherd. Neo-Marxism is misleading the children of God in the home, at school, and at work; yet the church is still restricting itself to dealing with old heresies and false religions of ancient days. Teaching the historic doctrines of the faith needs to be done. Fighting the old heresies of centuries ago needs to be done. Old heresies arise from the ashes constantly, and we need to be vigilant in fighting them. However, we have new heresies today that need to be confronted. I fear that our focus on the heresies of the past has taken away our ability to deal with the heresies of the present. One of those modern heresies is Neo-Marxism and its derivative CRT. To be a good shepherd of the flock, a pastor in the church must see the danger in this new religion, and he must be a voracious reader of books like those I have mentioned. He must be ready to proclaim the dangers of this new heresy, realizing that he will face a strong resistance for taking an unpopular stand.

Damage to Our Children. I am afraid that we have lost our tools of dominion. We have preached defeat and now we own it. We have taken hope for the future away from our youth, and then we are surprised when they leave the church for something else or just sit around with no purpose in life — or even join forces with the enemy. The modern church is a little like a high school football team when a player shows up for the first day for practice, and the coach tells him that the team is going to lose every game this season; but take heart, it will soon be over!

We need to show our children that we are marching to war, and that they have the privilege of marching with us. Give them something worth fighting for! And give them something to fight with! We teach our children the Catechism, but we do not prepare them to fight the battle against Wokeism which they will face as soon as they go off to college. Catechism training is good, but it is not enough.

If they go to work directly out of high school, they may have to take the DIE (Diversity, Inclusion, and Equity) test. If they go on into the military, they may be screened as a possible domestic terrorist, especially if they have been raised in a conservative church. It's like a ferocious giant is approaching our covenant children, and we have failed to teach them how to identify him, and we failed to give them the tools for fighting. I fear that many of them will be trodden down and trampled.

The woke movement has discovered the old tenets of the godly Puritans and secularized them (see the next chapter). They are on the march with optimism, seeking to capture our children, and continually capturing the high places in our land. The church sits around waiting for persecution or the rapture, or the world to end soon. Yes, God still does great work in the church despite our failures. However, I do believe it is fair to say that we have become irrelevant to the world in which we live.

Kingdom Builders. Kingdom-builders is a Christian identity that seeks to build God's Kingdom here on earth. Special people have gifts to build the church (preachers, elders, and teachers). But Kingdom-building also occurs outside of the church.

We have been told to take captive the Promised Land. With the ascension of Christ, the Promised Land has been extended from the borders of Palestine to the whole earth. We have been commanded to fight against the strongholds of the enemy. As Paul says in 2 Corinthians 10:5: "We are destroying speculations and every lofty thing raised up against the knowledge of God, and we are taking every thought captive to the obedience of Christ."

We have not had the faith to believe this can be done. Giants will fall if we advance with the cross of Christ before us, believing the promises of God. Onward Christian Soldiers! I fear that as the generation in the wilderness had to die, so the present generation may have to be removed from this earth prematurely so that God can raise up a new church generation not afraid to fight for the expansion of the Kingdom of God. We must claim, as did the Dutch Theologian and Prime Minister Abraham Kuyper, that every inch of ground on this earth belongs to Christ.

Kingdom-builders are to "occupy until I come" (Luke 19:13). "The God of peace will soon crush Satan under your feet (Rom 16:20)." The mustard seed becomes a great tree (Matt. 13:31–32). This is the joy of being in the army of God.

Conclusion

The Church at one time occupied the land here in America, as well as in Europe. However, we lost the land because we substituted "sojourner theology" (R2K) for kingdom-building theology.

As we were busy dreaming of heaven, and as we restricted the Kingdom of God to the church building, Neo-Marxism was preaching its own gospel of creating a utopia here on earth through equity enforced by the civil government. To do this they know that biblical Christianity must be forced into the shadows. It's time for the church to awaken from its dogmatic slumber and openly confront the heresy of this new religion that is not only directing the future of our nation, but is also capturing our children.

While the church in America is meeting, eating, and retreating, Neo-Marxism is preaching equity for all and is on the march seeking to capture every mind and every heart in this land. It has captured the universities, the media, and now is in control of the federal government. In America, when you control the federal government, you control just about everything.

However, there is hope. We must dismantle the myth of R2K Theology, Christian Pietism, and Escapism which control the church. We must see the Kingdom of God as encompassing all the institutions of life. Let us pray with all diligence as Jesus taught us in Matthew 6:10: "Your Kingdom come. Your will be done on earth, as it is in heaven." I will suggest a model for this in the next chapter.

Chapter 6
Christ is King

The Ascension of Christ

The Bible teaches us that when Christ ascended into Heaven, he was enthroned as King over all the world, alongside God the Father. He sits at the Father's right hand. This was a reward for his faithfulness in regard to his part in the accomplishment of redemption of the world. Therefore, Christ sits on his throne today and has been given the right to rule over all the world. We must recapture the same hope that David had when he said in Psalm 86:9 "All nations whom You have made shall come and worship before You, O Lord, and they shall glorify Your name."

The goal of the Kingship of Christ is ultimately for all the nations to bow before him as King. "God raised Him [Jesus] up to the heights of heaven and gave Him a name that is above every other name, so that at the name of Jesus every knee will bow, in heaven and on earth and under the earth, and every tongue will confess that Jesus Christ is Lord, to the glory of God the Father" (Phil. 2:9–11). This includes every nation on earth. Remember that a nation is basically defined as a people with a common border, a common language, and a common religion.

The Way to Victory

Jesus is in the process of subduing all things to himself. The means of accomplishing his goal of ruling all the earth is through the work of the church, as the church both preaches the gospel and teaches all the nations to obey all that Christ has taught us. Jesus guarantees success because he has all authority. As multitudes are converted from all the nations, each convert is to go back to his home, to his work, and to his community, and observe the commandments of God. Not everyone will be a Christian, but as Christians implement the laws of God in all of society, the people will be so receptive to this change that we will be able to call the nation a Christian nation.

The Importance of the Commandments for Society

The commandments of Christ that we are to teach the nations to obey are summarized in the Ten Commandments.[15] The first four commandments are a demand that every nation worship the God of the Bible alone (see below "The Fatal Flaw in the U.S. Constitution"). The fourth commandment provides a day of rest and worship which demonstrates the mercy of God to all mankind (and animals) because of the pains of toil in a fallen world.

The other six commandments demand of us the protection of our neighbors. We are to honor and cherish our parents. We must not harm our neighbor. We must not have sexual relations with our neighbor's wife or daughter (or even with our neighbor). We must protect the property of our neighbor. We must not bear false witness or lie about our neighbor. We must not covet. We must learn to be content with inequity in our lives. These are simple rules which, if followed, will provide for peace and prosperity in any nation.

The commandments of Christ are also found in the principles taught in the Old Testament. For example, before anyone can be convicted of crime in a court of law, there must always be two or three witnesses. Without witnesses there can be no convictions. This law was given to protect the accused. For witnesses who testify falsely, they shall be punished with the penalty that would have been due the accused. In other words, if you are a false witness in a murder case, then you will be put to death. This increases integrity in the court system. These are applications of the Ten Commandments. The Old Testament laws tell us in more detail how we must protect our neighbor. Indeed, the laws of the Old Testament are a wonderful source of specific principles that tell us how to love our neighbor.

---

[15] See R. J. Rushdoony, *Institutes of Biblical Law* (Vallecito, Calif.: Chalcedon Foundation, 1973), vol. 1.

The Civil Magistrate — A Minister of God

When the Christian Faith captures nations, we call this Christendom. The West (from Europe to America) has enjoyed living under the influence of Christianity for hundreds of years. One particular person of every nation who is called to protect the Christian nation and to enforce justice is the civil magistrate. He is to be a servant of the Lord Jesus Christ. The civil magistrate today includes town mayors, state governors, United States presidents, and all those on government councils and legislative bodies. Civil magistrates are to bless those who do good (as defined by God's law, of course), and to be an avenger on those who practice evil (as God's law defines evil, of course). If they fail in this, we should expect them to come under the judgment of God.

America as a Christian Nation

Although the United States has failed in many ways in being a Christian nation, yet at its beginning it was considered a Christian nation, both legally and in reality. By legally, I mean that the documents of our founding fathers stated it on paper. By this I am referring to the majority of the original States who had in their state constitutions requirements that all officeholders must have some commitment to the Christian Faith.[16] This was the time when States were more important than the federal government in Washington, D.C. This was before the Civil War.

By being Christian in reality, I mean that regardless of what was stated clearly on paper, the church (*de facto*) had so much influence, that we were a Christian nation anyway. In the South as recently as about 50 years ago, most businesses in small towns voluntarily closed early on Wednesdays so that their employees could attend Wednesday Night Prayer Meetings. There was no law on the books for this. It was done out of respect for the Christian Faith.

Indeed, the Civil War changed everything. It ended the rights and privilege of the states as self-governing bodies, and was the

---

[16] Gary DeMar, *God and Government* (Powder Springs, Geo: 1982-1986), 3 vols.

beginning of a centralized federal government that we have today. States are now obligated to implement the laws of the federal government, even if those laws contradict the laws of the state (as has been done in my own State of Tennessee). The Tenth Amendment to the United States Constitution restricting the powers of the federal government (and protecting the powers of state governments) has essentially been canceled.

The Fatal Flaw in the United States Constitution

As a result of the neo-Marxist movement in this country, I have been forced as a Christian and as an American citizen to re-examine our national history. Being trained as a Reformed theologian, I see things differently than most other people, even those who call themselves evangelicals. I'm amazed at how this research has changed my mind on numerous ideas that I had previously held as sacred.

I believe that since there was no religious test required for civil officeholders in the United States Constitution (Article VI, Clause 3), America officially became a polytheistic nation (everyone can believe in their own god).[17] At minimum, the Constitution should have required an oath to the Trinitarian God of the Bible for all office holders, as did the majority of States. This would not have sanctioned a National State Church, but it would have grounded our Constitutional Republic in the Christian Faith. It would have given the Supreme Court a reference point for issuing their decisions. Presently, there is no reference point except the vacillating opinions of men. States were already Christian, both legally and in reality, but the writers of the federal Constitution thought they could omit this in our national documents. This restrictive clause was a grave mistake.

---

[17] Gary North, *Conspiracy in Philadelphia, Origins of the United States Constitution* (Harrisonburg, Vir.: Dominion Educational Ministries, 2004). See: garynorth.com /philadelphia.pdf

The Fatal Flaw in the Declaration of Independence

After re-examining the Declaration of Independence, I now believe that its statement on equality was another grave error. After stating that it is self-evident that all men are created equal (which obviously on the face of it is not true), it goes on to say that all men are endowed by their Creator with certain unalienable rights, that among these are life, liberty, and the pursuit of happiness. After paying tribute to some generic creator, it defines equality in terms of the rights of man, and ultimately it defines the quality of life in terms of happiness. I call this American-branded equality. It does seem rather obvious that few men at the Constitutional Convention considered the slaves equal to the European Christian. Life is full of inconsistencies.

American equality in the Declaration was a secular attempt to define equality, and it has miserably failed. When we strayed in our founding documents from the God of the Bible as our Creator and Lawgiver, it only took about 200 years to see the fruit of such a major mistake. Today, we are in the midst of a Revolution that seeks to expel the Triune God and His law from every square inch of our nation. *Christianity is about to be canceled by Neo-Marxism.*

Others in the past have tried to define equality in a secular fashion. Modern left-wing progressives define equality in terms of equal outcomes for everyone. All men should share in the fruits of the labor of the group regardless of how much labor, capital, and risk each one has put into the building of society. Income and wealth should be redistributed evenly to all men. This is the cry for equity. It is Neo-Marxism. It is theft.

Modern right-wing conservatives define equality in terms of the equality of opportunity. We are told that even if we all begin from different starting points, if you work hard, keep your nose clean, and add a little ingenuity, then you can, not only be equal, but rise to the top. The opportunity is there. You can participate in the American Dream. Some have! We are told that this is the pathway to equality for all people. This has traditionally been called Capitalism.

However, it should be noted by Capitalists that starting points make a big difference in the pursuit of success. For example, a child who is raised in destitute poverty and who is from a dysfunctional home starts from a baseline far below others, and may never be able to catch up. A student in high school who scores a 400 on the SAT does not start at the same point as a student who scores 1600. Because of different starting points, not everyone can make it to the top (or even to the middle). What often happens is, apart from the Christian Faith, the have-nots become covetous of the haves, and this opens the way for the lure of Marxist equity.

Equality Under the Law

What then separates the biblical view of equality from the Declaration of Independence's deficient and inadequate view? As citizens of a nation, the Bible teaches that all men are equal indeed, but *equal* under the Law of God. This is what our forefathers failed to enshrine in the Declaration of Independence and in the United States Constitution. It may be implied in these documents, but it is not clearly stated.

Biblical equality demands that all men must be treated the same under the Law of God. There must be no partiality in judgment. "You shall do no injustice in judgment; you shall not be partial to the poor nor defer to the great, but you are to judge your neighbor fairly" (Lev. 19:15). This is biblical equality. Justice is the administration of the Law of God with its penalties by proper civil magistrates. Justice is color-blind. The Judge should act as if he is blindfolded. Justice does not consider economic status. Justice does not consider ethnicity. Justice applies equally across the board regardless of the individual, and regardless of his or her economic status or family connections. This is quite different from Marxist equality. This is quite different from either left-wing or right-wing economic equality. This is biblical equality.

Dealing with Guilt

Guilt is the result of breaking God's law. It is not some feeling (false guilt) that overcomes us because we have more material blessings than other people, or because we are a different color or a different nationality than other people. When used improperly, false guilt becomes a weapon to subdue the tender conscience. We cannot allow this to happen. Freedom from false guilt can only be maintained by understanding true guilt which is the transgression of God's Law, and the solution to true guilt which is redemption in Christ Jesus.

The Heresy of Polytheism

Polytheism is the belief that all gods are equal, and that anyone may worship any god he pleases. A polytheistic, multi-cultural society cannot long endure. Without a common God and Lawgiver, chaos or tyranny will eventually prevail. We denied the only King and Lawgiver in our national founding documents. We have allowed false religions to flourish in our midst. We believed that different races with different religions could all co-exist in peace. Different religions always bring their systems of law with them when they settle in a new country. Politics becomes the arena of the battle for power, rather than the administration of God's law equally to all men. The melting pot has become a boiling pot. We now have Muslims elected to the United States Congress, something years ago we never dreamed that could happen. We must understand the times in which we live.

Failure to Confess the Triune God

When Jesus was enthroned as King at the right hand of God the Father, he demanded worship not only from all individuals, but from all nations. Christianity is not a choice that man makes. Christianity is the demand of a sovereign God to worship him alone. "O Kings of the earth, kiss the Son, lest he become angry and you perish in the way" (Psa. 2:12). In our national documents, our forefathers failed to confess the Triune God as Lord over all, even over this nation. Although many of them were godly men, they avoided the declaration of the Triune God at the foundation of our nation. This was a grave error. They could not see the unintended consequences of their actions. *To avoid him is to void him*, and we are paying the price today.

Most States were originally Christian commonwealths. The Civil War ended the focus of government upon the States, and the Federal Government slowly became a tyrant. Since the U.S. Constitution does not legalize the Christian Faith, America became a secular state. Christianity held on for a long time, but that time has come to an end. It is being replaced by Neo-Marxism.

The Woke-movement — A Replacement Religion

The woke movement (Wokeism) is not merely a cultural or political movement. As I mentioned in chapter one, it is a religious movement. It is seeking to substitute itself as a new religion for the old Christendom that has permeated the western world for hundreds of years. As such, it has certain tools in its quiver that are propelling it to victory — a victory that may destroy the old Christian America. Our civilization is on the precipice of devastation, and Christians need to understand the enemy, and how they fight.

There are three fundamental tenets upon which the woke movement operates. They use a secularized version of the old Puritan theological beliefs which most of the church today has rejected. These powerful tools of Neo-Marxism are a twisted version of the old and godly Puritan Christianity. While the modern church has, as a whole, rebuffed the views that I espouse, the Neo-Marxist movement has adopted a corrupted version of them as instruments of warfare, and they have become very powerful and effective. Let me explain the essence of these secular tenets, how they duplicate the older Puritan Christendom, and how the Christian must fight against them.

1. A Hope for the Future
Millennial Views - Eschatology

The view of the future of Christianity on this earth before the Second Coming of Christ has been controversial. This area of study is called Eschatology (study of the end times). There are three main views defined in terms of the millennial period (described in

Revelation 20:2 as a 1,000-year period) which all agree is considered a "golden age" in regard to the influence of the Christian Faith on earth. The three views are each defined by a prefix that pinpoints when Christ will return in regard to the millennial period. A Pre-millennialist believes that Christ will return prior to the golden age. In this view, things will get worse on earth before Christ returns. It is an eschatology of pessimism. Amillennialists generally believe that we are in the golden age (from the Resurrection of Christ to the Second Coming). They too believe that things will get worse on earth before the Second Coming of Christ. It too is an eschatology of pessimism. Post-millennialists believe that Christ will return after the millennial period. Things will actually get better before Christ returns. It is an eschatology of optimism and hope.

Wokeism has adopted the post-millennialist paradigm, secularized it, and therefore believes that its future on this earth is bright. They are optimistic. They know that there will be a fight. There will be resistance. It will take time, but eventually they believe they will win. With a slow march through the institutions of our nation, capturing them one-by-one, the theology of Wokeism will become the new religion of America. LGBTQA+ rights, statism, control of the media, government schools who claim they own the children, Big Tech censorship, and the marginalization of Christians — all of these are their vision of the future of this country. This world is important and they intend to own it. This is one reason they are winning. Pessimistic eschatology is no threat to them.

The only antidote to this is a healthy, optimistic view of the power of the gospel not only to save men's souls, but to send those men out to capture the world by applying Christian principles to all of life. The Christian Faith does not stop with piety, but beginning with biblical piety, it becomes a great whirlwind that spreads over all the world and throughout every institution, as was evidenced in the Protestant Reformation. Such optimism used to belong to the church, but it has been rejected and now has become a basic tenet of Wokeism.

One of the many joys of celebrating Christmas is singing the old Christmas hymns like *Joy to the World*. Christians, please note the optimistic tenor!

> Joy to the World, the Lord is come!
> Let earth receive her King;
> Let every heart prepare Him room,
> And Heaven and nature sing,
> And Heaven and nature sing,
> And Heaven, and Heaven, and nature sing.
>
> Joy to the World, the Savior reigns!
> Let men their songs employ;
> While fields and floods, rocks, hills and plains
> Repeat the sounding joy,
> Repeat the sounding joy,
> Repeat, repeat, the sounding joy.
>
> No more let sins and sorrow grow
> Nor thorns infest the ground.
> He comes to make His blessings flow
> Far as the curse is found
> Far as the curse is found
> Far as the curse is found.
>
> He rules the world with truth and grace,
> And makes the nations prove
> The glories of His righteousness,
> And wonders of His love,
> And wonders of His love,
> And wonders, wonders, of His love.

I am afraid that the church has become very selective in the hymns that are used. Modern Christian music does not capture the theology of the old saints. Consider the optimistic and encouraging words of the Hymn "Jesus Shall Reign."

Jesus shall reign where'er the sun
Doth his successive journeys run;
His Kingdom stretch from shore to shore,
Till moons shall wax and wane no more.

To Him shall endless prayer be made.
And princes throng to crown His head,
His name like sweet perfume shall rise
With every morning sacrifice.

People and realms of every tongue
Dwell on His love with sweetest song;
And infant voices shall proclaim
Their early blessings on His name.

Blessings abound where'er He reigns:
The prisoner leaps to lose his chains,
The weary find eternal rest,
And all the sons of want are blest.

Where He displays His healing power
Death and the curse are known no more;
In Him the tribes of Adam boast
More blessings than their father lost.

Let every creature rise and bring
Peculiar honors to our King;
Angels descend with songs again,
And earth repeat the loud Amen.

We seldom sing hymns like this. The optimism of the coming reign of Christ on this earth before his Second Coming is missing in the modern church. It is now a major tenet of the woke movement.

2. The Covenant and our Children
To You and Unto Your Children

The idea of covenant can be defined in a multitude of ways. It is basically a contract. However, for many of us with children and grandchildren, it is a promise of God to be a God not only to us but also to our children and our children's children. When you think about the covenant you should think about your children and their future. It's about the children! The promises of God are to a thousand generations. The world does not end when you die. Most of us will leave children and grandchildren behind. Many generations will follow us. While heaven will be a joy for us, yet our focus and responsibility here now must also be on the generations that follow us.

Solomon said in Proverbs 13:22 that "A good man leaves an inheritance to his children's children, and the wealth of the sinner is stored up for the righteous." Christians are future-oriented because of the covenant. People of the covenant expect to see their children and grandchildren in church. We expect Christ to capture their hearts and make them love the Kingdom of God. We work hard to accomplish this by taking them to church, teaching them about Christ wherever we are, praying with and for them, and giving them a world-and-life view based on the Scriptures. We fight to keep our children in the Faith.

Wokeism is a secularized covenantalism and wants to capture your children. Your children are their target, few of them having any children of their own. Children are malleable and if we send them off to government schools and most modern universities, Wokeism believes it can convert them. They have been doing this for years, only Christians did not know it. Secretly, they have been capturing our children. As parents are beginning to see the reality of CRT, they are beginning to push back, but it may be too late.

3. The Kingdom and the Law
Kingdom-building with the Law of God

Kingdom-building theology is merely the application of God's law to society. Think political legislation! Even though the law does not justify us, yet for Christians who have been justified, it is a means to capture the world for Christ. The Ten Commandments (as applied in both the Old and New Testaments) must be foundational for any society if that society is to enjoy the blessings of God. The implementation of God's law is the medium of bringing blessing to all. The Bible speaks of issues surrounding economics, science, education, business, the arts, and all other areas of life. God's word relates to all the decisions I have to make every day in the workplace and at home.

Wokeism applies its own laws to society. They are imposing their law system on all of us via political legislation. Think of abortion and same-sex marriage. Every society will be ruled by some law. The question is whose law. They know this and they will use any means necessary to rule over all men. They will use federal, state, and local politics to impose their law system on everyone. The civil government will be weaponized to remove freedom from the people. "When the righteous thrive, the people rejoice; when the wicked rule, the people groan" (Prov. 29:2).

The Church needs to raise up a new generation of men who will go into all the various disciplines of life and conquer them for the glory of the Lord Jesus Christ. We have too many seminary students and not enough law students. Not enough business students. Not enough engineering students. We need godly men sitting on corporate boards, in the public universities, in Congress, and on the Supreme Court. I know this is not for everyone, but we need to be looking at our children and encouraging the brightest to pursue these callings. We have abdicated our place in the world, and we have let the woke-movement take control. Apart from those truly called to the ministry of the word, we need men studying the other disciplines rather than merely the systems of theology. We have departed the market place and now we are paying a heavy price.

CONCLUSION

A Quick Summary

The Protestant Reformation of the 1500s changed Europe. It challenged the status quo of not only the Roman Catholic Church, but it transformed every institution from civil government to other disciplines like education and medicine. It began with the doctrine of justification by faith alone, and it morphed into a great cultural movement.

The Reformation brought the Christian Faith to the shores of America. The United States has been a beneficiary of the blessings of Christendom. One only need look at the origins of such Ivy League Schools such as Harvard and Yale. Hospitals appeared everywhere bearing the names of Methodists, Baptists, and Presbyterians. The Bible was taught in the schools, not because it was good literature, but because it was the sacred book of the people of this nation. America could be described as part of Christendom.

However, as America grew older, the Reformation was lost. Mainline churches followed the latest heresies like a dog in heat. Dispensationalism (a type of pre-millennialism) denied the possibility of Christendom and replaced optimistic theology with pietistic escapism. Presbyterians, being proud of their heritage, soon were locked into the controversies of centuries ago, and were unable to detect other heresies just as dangerous in the modern day. Not being Dispensationalists, they substituted another defeatist eschatology with little hope for the future of their children and grandchildren. No secret rapture, but escapism still the same!

As both Europe and America drift toward Sodom and Gomorrah, a new religion is seeking to replace the influence of the Christian Faith. This new religion is Neo-Marxism. In this Conclusion, I will summarize some of the basic tenets covered in this book and how the church has responded.

First, the definition of CRT teaches us that if you are white, then you are guilty. You were born guilty and there is no need to discuss the matter. You are guilty of the oppression of not only the black race, but also of other minorities including homosexuals and transgenders. If you want to discuss the matter, the followers of CRT will scream in your face or burn down buildings in large cities.

The goal of CRT is not equality. Equality in a society only exists as citizens are equal under the law. The cry of CRT is *equity*. Equity includes a reference to wealth, whether it be defined in terms of monetary assets, position, or power. All three persons of the Trinity are equal, but they have different functions in the process of salvation. Inequity is a divine attribute of God himself. This provides a model for understanding equality and equity. CRT calls for the redistribution of wealth using the power of tyrants in the civil government, rather than recognizing and accepting the inequities that come from God.

Some theologians today are trying to deal with the CRT movement by denying that races are real. They are saying that race is simply a social construct. They are adopting a weapon of CRT to fight CRT. This will not work. Races do exist. The gospel is to be preached to all nations without discrimination.

God made the races, and there are variations among us. There has been inequity between the races, but inequity has nothing to do with white supremacy. The inequity that exists in the Black Race mainly comes from fatherless homes. The Christian Faith in the Black Community failed. The only hope for the Black Race is the recapture of a full-orbed Christianity that captures the family as well as the heart. Actually, this is the only hope for the White Race too.

Neo-Marxism is an attack on the nuclear family, or better said, an attack on the Christian family. Its strategy is to dismantle all Christian structures as outlined in the Bible. The church has failed to deal adequately with the Neo-Marxist movement. I do not believe that she is able to do so. This is one reason why I have written this book.

The church needs to study the religion of Neo-Marxism and prepare to battle this competitive religion in the world of ideas. A number of good books have already been written. The Evangelical and Reformed churches may be unable to engage in battle because they are so occupied with escapism and pietism. R2K is a prime example of this. We are so caught up in the heresies of the past that we cannot confront the heresy of our generation that the average person in the pew has to deal with every day. We must get out of our safe space and go into the world and confront our enemies with the whole counsel of God.

The battle in America today is not between political parties. It is not a battle between conservatives and progressives. *It is a religions war!* Historic Christianity is being attacked by a new religion called Neo-Marxism. It is a new form of the older Classical Marxism. Americans admire those who legitimately climb the social ladder through hard work and self-discipline, regardless of race. What we despise is a change in social structures that result from the tyranny of a civil government that seeks to redistribute wealth illegally. It is theft.

A Christian Nation (even defined by its legal documents) is not an anomaly in history. It is actually quite common. America began as a Christian nation if we view the nation as a confederation of States. The majority of State Constitutions were decidedly Christian.[18] The authors of the U.S. Constitution failed to follow the States in our national legal documents. This was a fatal flaw. We remained unofficially a Christian nation until the Civil War when the federal government usurped the powers of state governments. After that a shift in religions came slowly, but it is accelerating with great speed in our day.

The ultimate model for the rule of nations is found in the Ten Commandments, especially as it is revealed in its application in both the Old and New Testaments. The ceremonial laws of the Old Testament were fulfilled in Christ, but the general principles of the Law of God are still a benchmark for all peoples.

---

[18] See Gary North, *Conspiracy in Philadelphia, Origins of the United States Constitution* (Harrisonburg, Vir.: Dominion Educational Ministries, 2004), See: garynorth.com/philadelphia.pdf.

The only hope for a change in direction in this country is a reformation in the church. Just like the first Protestant Reformation, we need a revival of the gospel that changes culture.

Concluding Remarks

The ten spies of Israel had no faith in a God who would enable them to conquer the Promised Land. They were cowards, and God let them and their generation die in the wilderness. I fear that we may be repeating their folly. Even though we have the all-sufficient word of God, a Christ who sits on his throne, and the power of the Holy Spirit in our age, yet we still sound like the ten spies faint-heartedly talking about how big the enemy is.

God may let us die in the wasteland also, just like the generation of ten spies. And yes, this death may be through persecution, but not a persecution that is part of the essence of our calling as Christians, but a persecution that is due to our failure to believe in the promises of God. May God raise up a new generation that craves for the presence of the all-encompassing glory of God as he rules over all the nations and kings of the earth.

We are in spiritual warfare. The battle has never been purely political because politics is downstream from culture, and culture is downstream from religion. As religion goes in a nation, so goes the nation.

It's time to call CRT or Wokeism for what it is. It is another religion, another idol which must be resisted and overcome by the people of God, not with guns and swords, but with the power of the Holy Spirit by proclaiming the whole counsel of God. We are in the midst of a war. The consequences are serious.

For those who believe in the power of God to bring about a golden age before the Second Coming of Christ, we have much hope. People talk about how bad the world is today, and it is certainly "slouching toward Gomorrah." However, those who study history know that life has been much worse in the past. Most Christians I know today think that history began when they were born, and it will end when they die. They know very little about history.

The world was much worse before the Reformation of the 16th Century, but out of it came one of the greatest eras of Christianity that the world has ever seen. It can happen again.

Eschatology is considered a peripherical issue in almost every seminary today, but actually it is of such importance that it affects how a man preaches, how a man writes, and how a man lives. Sadly, it is a missing part in what I have called Selective Orthodoxy. An optimistic view of God's Kingdom on earth changes almost everything!

The next time you hear the word *equity* from BLM, from ANTIFA, the News Media, or the LBGTQA+ Community, from the federal government, or even from the church, remember: You are hearing the cry for a new religion that is seeking to replace the Christian Faith. The church must be awakened. We must not retreat from this battle. We have King Jesus sitting on his throne, the word of God, and the power of the Holy Spirit. "For the earth will be filled with the knowledge of the glory of the Lord as the water covers the sea" (Hab. 2:14). Victory belongs to us!

Other Books by Larry E. Ball

Blessed Is He Who Reads: A Primer on the Book of Revelation (2d. ed.: Chesnee, SC: Victorious Hope, 2015).

This book is intended to be a primer on the book of Revelation. A primer is a book for beginners, presenting the most basic elements of a field of study. It is a first step toward understanding something more complicated.

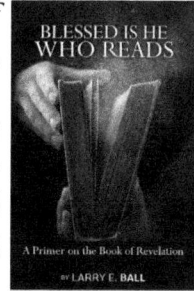

Unto You & Your Children: The Promises of The Covenant — A Primer (Chesnee, SC: Victorious Hope, 2016).

This book defines and illustrates the covenant as it appears in the Bible, and then demonstrates how the covenant affects our children as we raise them in the church. It also develops a justification for infant (covenant) baptism.

Available from
KennethGentry.com
Amazon.com